Hand in Hand

CONTENTS

ACKNOWLEDGMENTS

A thank you list can never be complete. So many people deserve acknowledgment here that I cannot name them all. Everyone listed has made a special contribution to my life and thus to this book, and I thank them all. I have divided them into three overlapping groups: personal, professional and exceptional.

Thanks to:

Personal
My power circle, composed of Austin Anton, M.F.C.C., Golda Clenendin, M.F.C.C., Tom Drucker, M.S., Shoshana Lane, and G. Roy Strassman, M.S., for supporting me in setting and reaching my goals, and for loving me through the rough spots.

My friends, including Joel and Manuela Adelman, Eliezer and Sandy ben Joseph, Carol Briseno, Rev. Camille Bertholet, Susan Breslow, Canary Conn, Ernest Del, J.D., Joy and Bob Dolce, Robert Felsette, Ray Gottlieb, O.D., Ph.D., Harvey Harrison, J.D., Alice Hoover, Joseph Kessler, Gurujit Singh Khalsa, Jas Want

Singh Khalsa, M.D., Siri Dharma Kaur Khalsa, Ellen Kesend, Donna David-Langer, M.A., Stu Langer, Jan Lueken, Ph.D., Brian Mack, Marsha Mayer, Majer Rubin, Marcia Seligson, Hank Shapiro, Sotiris Skrebas, Karen and deWayne Snodgrass, Heather and Les Sinclair, Orma Sullivan, Chet Wilson, Ph.D., Kenneth Wohlman, M.A., and anyone else who deserved acknowledgment and whom I have omitted, for forming a circle of support and love.

My family, for continuing to love me.

The staff of the SYDA Foundation, particularly Yamuna Marilyn Hershenson, M.S.W., Ganapati Joseph Buga, M.S.W., Durgananda Sally Kempton, Swami Shantananda, and Swami Brahmananda, for their helpful friendliness.

Werner Erhard, for creating the est training and related workshops, all of which have supported me in my ability to create magic in my life.

Reverend Gensho Fukushima, of Hofukuji Zen Monastery, who first taught me to meditate.

Reverends Corrie van Loon and Camille Bertholet of the OMNI Foundation, for their openness and love.

Professional
My clients, for sharing their lives with me.

My students, for asking questions.

All the teachers who helped me learn to love learning and to love language.

The staff of Celestial Arts, particularly Richard Baltzell, David Hinds, and Abigail Johnston, for their warmth, encouragement, and for doing their jobs so well.

William F. Strunk and E.B. White, for writing *The Elements of Style*.

Exceptional
My body, for being healthy and supporting me in my work. This book, for coming to me. All readers of my books, for their willingness to learn.

The positive forces that have guided me, protected me, and kept me safe until this day.

With special gratitude and love, this book is dedicated to Swami Muktananda Paramahansa and Bhagavan Nityananda, his teacher for all that they have done.

Hand in Hand

1

PSYCHIC PALMISTRY

The universe is in your hands. Your hands reflect every aspect of your physical, mental, emotional and spiritual life. Birth, death, growth, and the time your car broke down on the way to Lake Tahoe—all are reflected in your hands. Physically, your hands are the tools with which you touch and influence the world. Symbolically, they represent your creative power, their grace and coordination reflecting the divine essence within you right now.

Psychic Palmistry is a tool you can use to unlock the secrets of your own hands and experience more love and self-awareness. It is an outgrowth of traditional palmistry, which is the examination and intuitive interpretation of the lines, mounts, and marks on the hands.* In practicing psychic palmistry with others, you attune yourself to another person's character and energy while holding your own center. The more willing you are to receive insight and knowledge, the more insight and knowledge will seek you. A psychic palmreading is one of many contexts in which insight increases: it can happen to you.

The only requirements for learning psychic palmistry are an open mind and a willingness to see that you already have a sense of how to read people's hands. You're just refining your natural abili-

---

* For more information on traditional palmistry, see *The Hand Book* by Elizabeth Brenner, Celestial Arts, 1980.

ty. In the first few chapters, we'll cover all the aspects of basic palmistry. You'll learn about the hand shapes and the basic divisions of the hands as well as about the lines, mounts, marks and other features of the hands which tell you about a person's life and character in astonishing detail. You will also learn about a never-before-published field of palm-reading—reading the involuntary postures of the hands. By looking at the way a person holds her fingers when her hands are "at rest," you can see instantly how she uses her energy, how she blocks it, and how she can break free of her blocks. This is a particularly useful branch of palmistry because you can use it when glancing surreptitiously at the hands of friends (and enemies, too).

In the second half of the book you'll use the fundamental information from the earlier chapters to extend the applications of psychic palmistry far beyond the traditional. You will learn to analyze the hands to give you insight into *relationships.* That is, you will see how palmistry can help you avoid heartbreak and wasted time by showing you your potential partner's basic temperament, attitudes toward emotional involvement, strength of will, sexual drive and the number of marriages he or she is likely to have. If you are looking for a new relationship, this chapter will help you zero in on the appropriate person; if you are in close relationships already, compatibility palmistry will help you understand your loved ones better. Moreover, you're sure to enjoy holding the hands of the people closest to you—that's how a lot of those friendships got started, after all.

In the closing chapters, you'll learn to use all the practices and information from the first parts of the book as a springboard for greater self-awareness and satisfaction in all areas of your life— even beyond holding hands.

I'll use the word "psychic" frequently in this book; there will also be references to the "intuitive" mind. To avoid confusion, here are general definitions of these words. "Intuitive" refers to the nonlinear, visualizing functions associated with the right side of the brain. The intuitive mind is the part of you that gets feelings, hunches and premonitions and that synthesizes many bits of information instantly into accurate conclusions. It is your gut feeling and is the foundation of "higher consciousness," too. Everyone has intuition, although some use it more than others.

"Psychic" awareness is the natural extension of intuitive awareness. It involves a clear comprehension of the information perceived by the intuition and usually produces more detailed information than the intuition alone. For example, it would be intuitive to have a feeling that something is wrong at your friend's house, but it would be psychic to know that the stove had set the curtains on fire and three fire engines were rushing to the scene. Psychic awareness goes beyond the speechless vision of the right brain; it taps into the energy fields around oneself, others and events and then filters insight into the verbal mind, making them comprehensible.

The word "psychic" also refers to certain unusual powers, including telepathy (knowing others' thoughts), precognition (knowing future events), psychokinesis (moving physical objects solely by the power of the mind) and psychometry (knowing about circumstances surrounding an object only by touching the object itself). While these abilities might seem exotic at first, they become plausible when we observe that the entire universe—physical, mental, emotional and spiritual—is composed of energy. Every day we see energy change form and intensity. Light becomes heat, water produces force, even the food we eat becomes physical energy (or fat!). Energy changes constantly according to the task at hand. "Psychic" powers are different ways of using energy, just as running a toaster or lighting a movie marquee are different ways of using electricity.

Even though psychic abilities are part of the natural scheme of things, most of us feel a little uneasy at the prospect that someone might use her psychic powers around us or at the thought that we might have psychic powers ourselves. This uneasiness is a product of our cultural conditioning, and it can be overcome if we are willing to look at it dispassionately.

Observe yourself now. What images does the word "psychic" call up in you? Say out loud, "I am psychic." How do you feel? Notice especially any changes in your breathing or in the pit of your stomach. How do you feel about being psychic? It's not necessary to do anything with your fears and beliefs except to flush them out and look at them. The more aware we become of our own patterns and emotions, the less power they have over us. Once we state our willingness to be aware of fears and beliefs, we will become aware of them at just the pace we can handle. If we let them rise, and look at them without adding or subtracting anything, eventually they'll leave us alone.

To be psychic, we must be *receptive*. The information we want is already available to us. Once we trust that this is so, we can receive psychic insights with no effort at all. The more effort we feel when doing psychic readings, the more we are interfering with our natural flow of intuitive knowledge. There are times when rational, assertive thought is appropriate: the middle of a psychic reading is not one of them. With practice, you will learn to voluntarily suspend your rational mind so that the reading can flow spontaneously. After that you can re-engage that rational side while you interpret and communicate the information you received. This is like shifting gears on a car; the more you practice, the easier it gets. With more practice you'll reach a point where your intuitive mind speaks through your rational mind and your rational mind is constantly inspired by your intuition. That is, you will integrate the different sides of your mind.

Psychic Pushups: Big Deal

Many books and classes are available which claim to make you more "psychic." Some of them work. If you really want to fly, walk on water, get a new stereo by magic or meet the movie star of your dreams, you might be able to do it by forcing your psychic powers to work for your personal desires. But so what? These miracles are small potatoes. You might get what you want, but you might get something else as well, and that something else you might not like. The ability to produce results with psychic powers does not guarantee that you'll be happy. Furthermore, the ability to produce results with psychic powers does not guarantee that you'll be a nice guy. In fact, some people use it to become downright nasty. Please do not think that bending spoons or casting spells are the highest spiritual achievements you can attain. It's much more fun to aim for awareness of the love within everything and let psychic powers come where they may.

The pursuit of psychic powers is unnecessary, because everyone is potentially psychic. If you hold still, psychic abilities will come to you like a fawn in the woods. Pursuing them is like stomping through the woods bawling, ''Here fawn! Here fawn!'' If you ever can pin it down, it might bite you. By holding still and maintaining a gentle, receptive attitude, you create the situation in which the fawn willingly comes to you. Venison eaters disregard this metaphor. Everything you want to know is available right now. Are you listening?

There are three ways in which people become actively psychic: through a natural gift, through training in psychic skills, and as a byproduct of the increased awareness that comes from meditation and spiritual practice. No matter how any member of these groups became psychic, all of them get better at it when they practice doing it. Although the first two groups might slide by without joining the third (meditating) group, they would benefit from joining it. Those who seek psychic powers in the apparent absence of a natural gift should pay special attention here. If you want to be psychic, *meditate*. Meditation expands all our abilities at a natural pace.

One of the many reasons to develop psychic powers as byproducts of a gradually awakening consciousness is that using psychic powers responsibly requires good mental health, and meditation eventually results in excellent mental health. (Physical health usually improves through meditation, too.) Good mental health means having the flexibility to adapt to change along with the stability to maintain equilibrium in the midst of that change. And those are qualities that you need if you want to do psychic palmreadings. Schizophrenics often have psychic or mystical visions—their problem is that they can't tell the difference between their visions and everyday reality. Extremely weak and disturbed people are unable to channel and use their psychic energy productively so it shoots through them like sparks shooting from a frayed wire.

Through time, meditation cleanses and stabilizes the mind. If you start as a schizophrenic you may still have shaky moments, but you'll find an essential calm that makes the shakiness less like an earthquake and more like a minor tremor. If you begin where most of us do, with a slight malaise which shows we feel something's missing from our lives, and if you persevere, you will undoubtedly see dramatic improvements in every aspect of your life, including but not limited to the psychic.

Although there is no direct relationship between the practices of meditation and of palmistry, I know that my accuracy as a palmist and counselor is directly related to the time I've spent practicing meditation. During the last several years, new arenas of intuitive awareness opened up for me through some spiritual or meditative practices. Having learned to concentrate and remove distractions through meditation, I can now read palms calmly with blenders buzzing and cars roaring by. Of course, this might not be something you'd want to do, but still, it's an achievement. The comments in this book come from my personal experience. Meditation works, and it does more than make you psychic.

Energy Fields

When Albert Einstein was asked to describe relativity as briefly as possible, he replied, "Something's moving." And he was right. The universe is energy in motion, appearing in various densities, frequencies and forms. Everything has a field of energy around it. The human energy field has been studied intensely, by yogis and mystics for millennia, and by modern researchers for about one hundred years. While each group describes its obvservations from within its own conceptual framework, they agree on certain basics. The human aura surrounds the body as a constantly shifting mantle of light. It can have many colors, depending on the health and emotional state of the individual. It can extend as a powerful projection around the body or be raggedly contracted to the area just over the skin. When a person dies, the aura goes away, perhaps to return another day. It is through the aura that many "psychic" experiences take place. The lines and mounts of the hands reflect changes within the aura. When we hold the hands and close our eyes to feel the energy from the other person, we are picking up her energy field as projected through the hands.

Energy and the Hands

You will use a variety of talents when practicing psychic palmistry. These include close observation, sensitive touch, receptive awareness, compassionate speech, and the ability to sit still long enough to look over someone's hands. The psychic aspects of palmistry include feeling the relative energy flows on the right and left sides of the body, interpreting subtle variations in the color and temperature of the hand, and occasionally receiving detailed factual information about people while in a state of deep receptivity. All these activities, from simple observation to deep trance, arise from the same source—universal energy. You are using cosmic energy to read this book right now Cosmic energy is digesting your last meal. Cosmic energy did your dishes last night. In fact, everything you've ever seen, been, or done was made fundamentally of cosmic energy. The universe is nothing but cosmic energy playing dress-up.

Cosmic energy is in the palms, and cosmic energy will help you read the palms. All in all, cosmic energy is great stuff, and there's a lot of it around. What's called "psychic insight" is just an extension of the insight that guides you not to amble slowly in front of a speeding train. It is available to you once you set aside your resistance and let it come to you.

The hands are a particularly wonderful focus for your insight and energy because the signs on the hands are so clear. People sometimes wonder why we read the hands instead of the nose or the feet, and the answer is that there is no reason. Any part of the body reflects the whole. Your every cell contains the information necessary to reproduce your entire body. We read the hands because so much information is concentrated there, they're easy to get at, and they're fun to hold. Try telling someone you want to hold her nose and see how far you get.

Polarities Right and Left

Before going any further, we will settle once and for all the question of which hand to read. Read both. There are two ways to look at the meaning of the two hands: from the standpoint of handedness (right- or left-handed) and from the standpoint of polarities. Each approach has certain values and you can use both of them in your readings.

When doing a reading based solely on observation, it's easiest to look at right and left from the standpoint of "handedness" or hand dominance. Nearly everyone is either right-handed or left-handed; even people who claim to be ambidextrous tend to favor one side over the other. About 89% of people are naturally right-handed. In traditional palmistry, the dominant hand reflects the life the person is actually living, and the nondominant hand shows the past or the innate potential. By comparing the two hands you can see the relationship between the person's potential and her experience.

A woman once came to me who illustrated this point exactly. She was wealthy, successful, happily married and satisfyingly employed. By every standard, she had it all together. She told me that people who met her often envied the apparent ease with which she managed her life. Her dominant hand confirmed the fact that she was stable and well-adjusted—the lines were clear, mounts full and firm, quadrants well balanced and the overall tone of the hand was healthy. A glance at her other hand, however, showed the long road she'd traveled to become the "effortlessly happy person" that she was. The lines on her left hand were uniformly weak and chained. Even the mounts looked insipid. These natural weaknesses were the foundation of her happiness and strength. Her nondominant hand showed the frailty that she could have allowed to run her life. Her dominant hand showed that she had used her weaknesses and difficulties to advantage, forging them into an ever greater stability and an ability to create happiness regardless of her circumstances. By comparing what the person is with what she might have been, you gain insight into her character. Has she turned weaknesses into strengths or strengths into weaknesses?

Once in a while you meet someone whose nondominant hand is full of clear lines and powerful energy and whose dominant hand is a 97 pound weakling. This means she had everything going for her and somehow she blew it (at least for the moment). This reduction in natural power stems initially from some barrier within the individual. Consciously or unconsciously, she has been unwilling to let things be so good, and she has allowed her inner barriers against growth to become iron walls. Of course, she probably does not see her situation this way. She may think her life doesn't work because she's sick, or because her mother toilet-trained her too early, or because of the Federal Reserve Board. And it may be true that she is sick, her mother didn't have a way with kids and the Reserve Board has a reactionary monetary policy. But for someone with a positive attitude, all these factors would be challenges for growth, not reasons for stagnation. She has a right to believe her story, so don't contradict her directly. What she's telling you is true for her. You can, however, remind her that she is more than the collection of incidents in her life and that her thoughts have a direct effect on her experience. You can encourage her to look at herself more clearly, and trust that whenever she is willing to look at what stands between her and her power, her power will be released.

Polarities

A more comprehensive way to look at the right and left sides is from the standpoint of *polarities*. A polarity is one of two opposite principles, poles or tendencies. For example, the earth has the North Pole and the South Pole, and both chemistry and physics are based on an understanding of the relationship between positive and negative electrical poles. Living systems also have polarities. In ancient Indian and Chinese philosophy as well as in modern polarity theory, the right side is associated with the masculine, active or positive pole and the left side is linked to the feminine, passive or negative pole. In Chinese nomenclature, the right side is *Yang* and the left side is *Yin*. It's essential to understand both sides of an individual when reading her hands, so we read both hands.

The universe is composed of interacting polarities. Light and dark, positive and negative, masculine and feminine—look closely at any object or event and you can see how the dynamic interplay of these two forces creates one ever-changing motion. Atoms are held together by the interplay of positive and negative electrical charges; this pattern repeats itself throughout the chain of creation. It is also replicated in patterns of consciousness. Each of us has both an active side and a passive one, an outer persona and an inner life, busy times and quiet times. The relationship between these two sides forms the basis of most of our actions. Do you consider yourself an introvert or an extrovert? More a leader or more a follower? More a man or more a mouse? These and many other pairs of characteristics are examples of the active and passive polarities. (By the way, you can be more a woman than a mouse, too.)

Regardless of whether a person is right-handed or left-handed, or male or female, the right side of the body is considered "masculine" and the left side is considered "feminine." This is not some sexist plot to claim that women are passive and men are active.

These names have been used for millennia to describe the two basic aspects of life. If you reflect on your own experience you will see that every person has both a masculine and a feminine side. The theory of polarities simply systematizes what all of us can observe. Imbalances between the two polarities cause many physical, mental and social problems. How many times have you been active when you should have been passive or stayed passive when you should have been active? Don't start counting now or you may never finish the book. The polarities can be balanced so that they are in constant, dynamic equilibrium, provided we are first willing to see how they have been out of balance. As we progress into the area of psychic palmreading, you will see how you can read the energy flows from both sides of a person's body simply by holding her hands.

Energy flows through the hands from the base, near the wrist, to the fingertips. From the base of the hands rise the primary energies of the physical body and the unconscious mind. These raw powers are filtered as they rise through the hands, being transformed into our mental, physical and emotional faculties. This energy changes form just as electricity changes form between the power plant and the household.

With our hands we grasp the world, touching, communicating and implementing our will. Since the hands serve us in all our dealings with the world, they also reflect changes in our lives with great accuracy and speed. As a psychic palmist you will be more concerned with the changes and trends in the hands (and therefore the life) than with the way things are right now. Einstein was right. Something is moving. Us.

Look at your hands now. Notice the rounded area near the base of the thumb: it's the Mount of Venus, and it reflects your physical stamina and sensuality. Feel it with the fingers and thumb of your other hand. Is it soft? Hard? Full? Flat? Get that feeling now and remember it. Then sometime in the next few days, especially if you're feeling either very tired or very relaxed, feel your Mount of Venus again. You will notice a difference. The mounts of the hands can change quite rapidly, giving us a moment by moment view of the altering energy flows within us. (The lines on the palms can also change, but they do so more slowly.)

Just as there is no real duality between mind and matter, so there is no real break between the rational and the intuitive sides of our consciousness. They are polarities of the everchanging energy we call life. We need them both. Our hands take sides, too, and we wouldn't want to make do with only one of them.

As you explore the hands and your mind, move freely from the analytical to the intuitive sides. Don't hang on to either mode and whatever's appropriate will arise. You need not be any more or less psychic than you already are. Love yourself exactly as you are, recognizing the divinity within you, and the experiences you desire will seek you—unless what you desire is to be older, younger, taller, shorter, or a begonia.

2

BEGINNING HANDS

Look at your hands. What catches your attention first? How would you describe them? How do you feel about them? Would you take them home to mother, or are they just another part of your body? Whether you realize it or not, you are responding to many aspects of the hands when you form your feelings about them. These include their color, texture, temperature, flexibility, dampness and the state of the nails as well as the balance among the four quarters of the hand. The condition of the lines, mounts and marks also affects you. In addition to all this information, you are responding to the thoughts and beliefs about hands in general, and your hands in particular, which you picked up early in life. You can refine your natural feeling for the hands if you enjoy learning about them and trust your intuitive sense.

It is best to begin studying the hands by getting a sense of them without looking for information and by establishing an atmosphere of trust. Let your eyes wander over your own hands or those of a friend and see what parts or lines stand out. Cradle your friend's hands in your own, support them as you would a baby's head and do not cover them with your own. You might feel inclined to run your fingers or thumbs over the palms to sense the skin texture or to enjoy the feel of the mounts. A hand reading can be an exciting and intimate encounter if both people are open to experiencing the love within each other's unique characters. You set the tone for the reading by your attitude and the way you treat the hands, so hold them with love and relax as you scan them. Establishing an ambience of love and respect through your touch is the first requirement when reading the hands. Now for some basic mechanics.

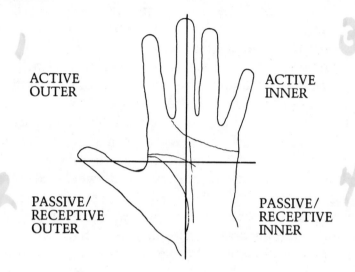

ACTIVE
OUTER

ACTIVE
INNER

PASSIVE/
RECEPTIVE
OUTER

PASSIVE/
RECEPTIVE
INNER

The Four Quadrants

The first and most basic division of the hands is into *quadrants*. Draw an imaginary line (or an ink one if you really want to) down the center of your third finger. Now draw another line horizontally across the palm, midway between the base of the thumb and the base of the index finger. You have now divided your hand into four "quadrants." The area above the horizontal line (toward the fingers) represents the *active* aspect of character and the area below it (toward the wrist) represents the *passive/receptive* aspect. The passive/receptive energy is the foundation of the active: action always originates from stillness.

The area on the thumb-side of the vertical line represents the *outer-directed* energy, and the area on the pinky-side represents the *inner-directed* energy. These four terms will become clearer to you as we explore the quadrants further.

If you look at the illustration on this page, you will see the four quadrants labelled according to the combination of the two axes. The upper half of the hand is divided into two quadrants: the *active/inner* and the *active/outer*. The bottom half is divided into the *passive/receptive/inner* and the *passive/receptive/outer* quadrants. Look at the illustration again and then refer back to your own hands; see these quadrants in yourself. Once you can see them in your own hands it will be easier to read them in the hands of others. The quadrants are simple to learn if you recall that the area above the horizontal line is active and the area below the line is receptive, and that the thumb-side of the hand is outer-oriented while the pinky-side is inner-oriented.

The basic priorities of the person's life are shown by the relationship among the quadrants. The lower parts of the hands contain the energies of physical stamina and the unconscious mind. The upper, active energies are more refined. The four quadrants represent the four major directions a person's energy can take. Some people are more comfortable in the north, others prefer the south, and still others can be comfortable anywhere. Ideally, all four quadrants will be equally balanced, none seeming particularly weak or strong. If a person has strong tendencies in any direction, a glance at the quadrants will tell you so instantly. A business—or outer world—dominated person will have much more tension and emphasis in the active/outer quadrant. Similarly, if someone is underdeveloped in any area of life, the quadrant associated with that area will appear drained. Here are more specific explanations of each quadrant. We will follow them clockwise around the hand.

The *active/outer* quadrant is composed of the thumb, the index finger and half of the third finger. The thumb represents the personal will, the index finger represents self-confidence and ambition, and the third finger helps distinguish between right and wrong. Will power, self-confidence, leadership and arbitration ability, all are active qualities oriented more toward the world outside oneself than toward the world within. Very ambitious, extroverted people frequently have dominant active/outer quadrants in which the thumb and the index finger are tense and hyperextended.

The *passive/receptive/outer* quadrant contains the mount at the base of the thumb, which is also called the Mount of Venus. It is the storehouse of physical stamina and sensuality. A thick round mount here shows a sturdy constitution and great resistance to disease.

A Czech man with a passive/receptive outer quadrant like a ham hock once complained to me that he had never gotten a day off for being sick. He envied people who got sick because they got to stay home and watch TV all day. This quadrant needn't look like Mount Fuji, but it shouldn't be Death Valley, either. Ideally it is firm and full in proportion to the rest of the hand, yet not so overpowering that the person can only think about exercise and sex.

The *passive/receptive/inner* quadrant is the same as the Mount of Luna, which is below the "equator" of the palm, on the pinky side. Luna represents the intuitive, unconscious mind. In people who are deeply involved with spiritual or psychic pursuits this quadrant either stands out or is deeply etched with lines. A desiccated passive/receptive/inner quadrant shows poverty of imagination. People with dry Luna mounts can hardly imagine how their own mothers look.

The *active/inner* quadrant contains half of the third finger and all of the fourth and fifth fingers. The fourth finger represents self-expression and creativity, and the fifth finger represents communication, especially verbal communication. The third finger is the "middle man" of the hand, arbitrating between the inner and outer sides of the personality as well as creating standards by which to judge between right and wrong. One rarely finds the active/inner quadrant strongly developed, since it represents a rare enthusiasm for sharing one's true inner self with the world. Only the devoutly self-expressive have hands in which this quadrant dominates.

You are more likely to find this quadrant in collapse. When a person has shut down his connection to the inner self, the active/inner quadrant wilts. Whenever you see the fourth and fifth fingers habitually held bent, you know the active/inner quadrant is weak. This means that the person hesitates to express what is going on inside himself.

The Hand Flex

After you have gotten a sense of the quadrants, continue to explore the hand by noticing its flexibility and tension. This is one of the simplest parts of hand reading. If the hand is flexible, that is, if it bends easily back and forth when you flap it around, the person is adaptable and flexible. If the hand is like cement from tip to wrist, guess what is so about the person: he is rigid, authoritarian and stiff. If the hand is too flexible, that is, if it has mushy skin and tapioca bones, then the person is a little too flexible. He is too willing to succumb to the desires of other people and the vagaries of fate. After gauging the tension of the whole hand, flex each of the fingers back and forth. Make a mental note of which fingers seem stiffer than the others; you will learn to interpret the tension patterns when we get to fingers.

Long Live the Red, White and Blue . . . Hands

Color and dampness of the hands also give you clues about character. If they are green and damp, the person has a reptilian character. Don't let him near your fly collection. Other than that, there are two types of color in the hands. They are the color of the hands themselves, and the color of the lines. In this section we are only talking about the color of the hands, so don't get excited yet about that purple line. A red tone in the hand indicates a strong but volatile nature, and sometimes marks a tendency to hypertension and overeating of rich food. Pale skin indicates a cool disposition and poor circulation. If you pull the fingers of a pale hand back, away from the palm, and the lines are blue instead of pink it may indicate anemia. This can be confirmed by a blood count, which must be prescribed by a physician. If the hands are yellowish, the person is either heavily calloused (physically, not mentally), jaundiced (physically, not mentally), or has been drinking way too much carrot juice.

Putting a Damper on the Hands

Sweatiness and dryness are additional sources of information from the hands. Perspiration is basically regulated by the endocrine system. TV commercials notwithstanding, sweating is good for you, and can even be fun. When you are nervous or hot, you automatically start to sweat, which cools you down. Once you are cool and relaxed, the sweating stops. No sweat. If your thyroid gland is overactive, the hands, along with the rest of the body, will sweat incessantly; if it's on a permanent vacation, the hands will be doughy, dry and sausage-shaped. Your thyroid gland is probably as normal as can be, so unless you have very severe symptoms which you had noticed before you picked up this book, please don't worry about it.

Much of the interpretation of dampness is based on common sense. If you have a fever your hands will be hot and dry. If you're in the bathtub they will be hot and wet. And if you spray them with the right deodorant, they will be soft and dry. The really complex rules of palm reading apply to environmental temperature. When you are hot, so are your hands. When you are cold they keep you company, too. In general, a slight dampness of the hands shows that the person is a little nervous at the prospect of having his hands read. Wouldn't you be?

A Free Sample-Reading

Now suppose Mr. Olson asks for your sage advice about his hands. They are red and he isn't sunburned. You try to bend the hands and find them stiff as boards. Not only that, they are slightly sweaty and his Saturn finger is even stiffer than the rest of that stiff, stiff hand. Well, Watson, what do you make of it? Surely your lightning wit has already told you that the red hand held rigid shows a volatile nature under tight control, the sweatiness shows nervousness at the prospect of being found out, and the super stiff Saturn finger shows the probable root of the whole problem: overdeveloped rules of right and wrong. Conclusion: unable to accept his own volatility, he stiffens up and probably becomes quite critical of those who shake their booties with the enthusiasm he represses in himself. You cannot cha-cha with him in impunity. Note that you deduce all this with nary a glance at a line or a mount.

Gods, Planets, and Palms

Imagine you have just moved to a new city. The Welcome Wagon lady has not arrived, and she probably never will. So you decide to find your way around by yourself. One of the first things you will want to learn is what you are likely to find in the different parts of town. Once you know the character of different districts, you know where to go when you are looking for something in particular. Like cities, the hands have "districts." Once you learn your way around them you will be ready to learn more details about them. On the hands, these details include the mounts, the hand shape and the lines. After you master all the basic information about your new home you will be able to find your way around without a tour guide.

Mount Olympus In Your Hands

Every major part of the hand has a name. These names are not random, but are actually code words for the type of energy that is channeled through each part of the hand. So don't start calling your pinky "Harold." Remember that the hands are microcosms that reflect the macrocosm of your life. Thus, every type of energy and behavior pattern has a location in the palm. Well, maybe you can imagine some that would be censored from the hand, but all the essentials are covered. By comparing the different parts of the hand, you see the strengths and priorities in the life of each individual.

All names for parts of the hand come from Greek and Roman mythology. The gods and goddesses of ancient times are far more than characters in fairly tales. They represent aspects of humanity crystallized into archetypal forms. For example, Jupiter, king of the gods, represents the regal aspect of man. He acts out both the positive and the negative aspects of exerting power over others— the positive when making wise and compassionate decisions, and the negative when turning virgins into cows because they won't have dinner with him. Stories about Jupiter address the Jupiter within each of us, that energy which represents *self-confidence, leadership, ambition, executive ability and sometimes religious leadership. Jupiter is associated with the index finger.*

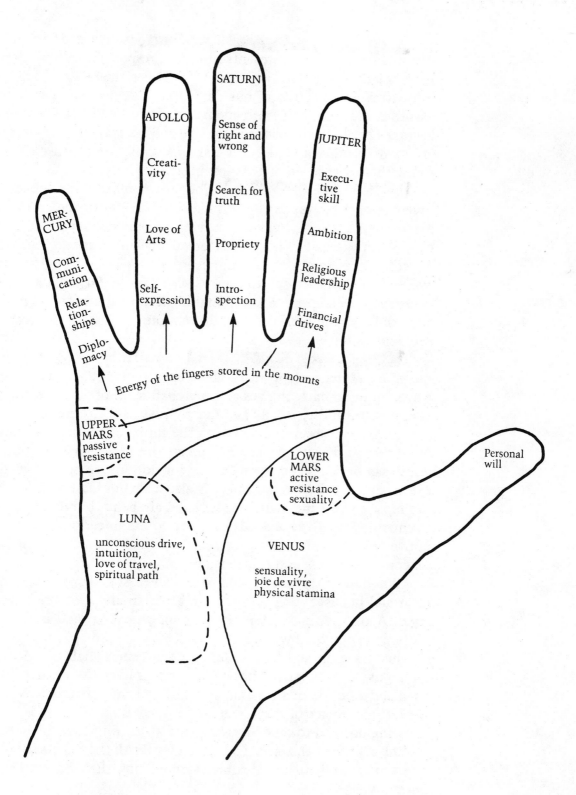

SATURN

Sense of right and wrong

Search for truth

Propriety

Intro-spection

APOLLO

Creati-vity

Love of Arts

Self-expression

JUPITER

Executive skill

Ambition

Religious leadership

Financial drives

MER-CURY

Communi-cation

Rela-tion-ships

Diplo-macy

Energy of the fingers stored in the mounts

UPPER MARS
passive resistance

LOWER MARS
active resistance
sexuality

Personal will

LUNA

unconscious drive,
intuition,
love of travel,
spiritual path

VENUS

sensuality,
joie de vivre
physical stamina

Saturn is associated with the middle finger. The god Saturn is a judge, so his finger represents morality, responsibility and *ideas of right and wrong.* He also mediates between the introverted and the extroverted aspects of our character. The positive aspect of Saturn is the search for truth and moral action. When the positive becomes excessive it turns to negative and takes the form of over-criticism, rigidity and perfectionism. You just can't please a person with an overdeveloped Saturn finger.

Apollo rules the ring finger. Phoebus Apollo, god of the sun, inventor of the lyre, patron of medicine, creator of the arts and master of all beauty, lives within you. So why don't you let him choose your drapes? This energy creates beauty, art and most of all, self-expression. Although not everyone is a professional artist, everyone does have a self to express. Self-expression is what gives content to our communication, making it more than another pretty sound. On the hands, *Apollo in the fourth finger is the god of self-expression.*

The fifth finger is named Mercury. Small in stature, but not in meaning, Mercury represents *verbal communication.* He is the patron of diplomats, thieves and merchants, all of whom have in common the ability to talk fast in a tight situation. A strong Mercury finger thus represents skill in the forms of communication. Note that it doesn't necessarily mean the person has anything worth saying, but even when he's saying nothing, he sounds good. A well-developed Mercury finger is also a sign of tact. Mercury is the most significant finger on the hand after the thumb, because so much of our lives depends on clear communication. It is best not to wear rings on this finger, as they block the flow of energy for communication and relationships.

When Mercury joins Apollo to form well-stated expressions of clear and honest thought, the skies brighten and everyone saves time. Apollo without Mercury is a song unsung, and Mercury without Apollo is all wind.

Just as each god had a place in the central hall on Mount Olympus, so each energy has a place in our lives. All of them are good and all of them are equal, so let us welcome them all. When we let one aspect of ourselves lord it over the others, it is like allowing one god to take up two chairs at the dinner table on the Mount. Don't let the other gods stand for it. All the fingers should be equally straight and flexible, symbolizing their balance and harmony.

The Offset Thumb, or How We Beat the Monkeys

The thumb is the only finger which is not named after a god, because it is uniquely human. It represents the personal will. Its shape tells you about the person's basic character, how he makes decisions and how firmly he carries out his plans. Its posture tells you his mood and general attitude toward life. Its absence tells you he got on the wrong side of a sharp object early in life. Reading the thumbnail gives you an immediate overview of the health. Whoever coined the phrase "a thumbnail view" wasn't kidding. One swift glance at the thumb can sum up the whole character. So if you don't want to be found out, keep yours in your mouth.

The size and setting of the thumb are also significant. Short thumbs end near the base of the index finger, and long thumbs extend beyond the middle joint of the index finger. All other thumbs are moderate. Tradition has it that great men are marked by their enormous thumbs. Voltaire and Newton are often cited as examples of geniuses who could be seen for miles when they signalled "thumbs up." This is contradicted by statistical studies which show that high achievers are just as likely to have normal length thumbs as long ones. Nevertheless, someone with a long thumb is more likely to achieve high goals than someone with a stilted deformed thumb. Tiny thumbs often show weak will and poor character.

Before you proclaim a thumb as long or short, notice where it is set into the hand. A long thumb set low in the hand is not a short thumb. If the thumb seems submerged into the hand, the person is absorbed in the passive energies of life. This can make him warm but not terribly expressive. If it is a little higher than that but still set low, the person draws more energy from the Mount of Venus than usual, so he's warm-hearted and glad to do favors when he can. Some palmists claim that a high-set thumb signifies a dynamic, extroverted personality. However, monkeys and idiots also have high thumbs. On a so-so hand, the high thumb shows stubbornness and arrogance. On a strong hand it means great personal strength and likelihood of success.

The thumb is based in the passive/receptive/outer quadrant (a.k.a. the Mount of Venus), which means that it is rooted in the great power of externally directed physical energy. That makes it the Jack LaLanne of the hand. This mount sets the tone for all the outer oriented action of the hand, so the finger that springs from it

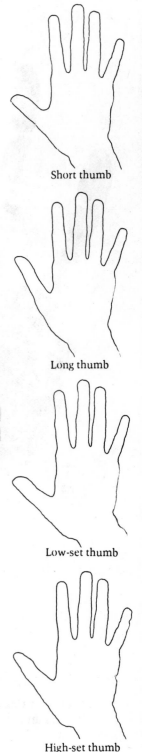

Short thumb

Long thumb

Low-set thumb

High-set thumb

Compare the long fingers and long thumb of the hand above to the short fingers and thumb of the hand to the right.

deserves special attention. The two upper joints of the thumb show how this powerful energy is set into motion.

Spatulate thumb

The middle (second) joint shows reasoning ability, or an ability to get what one wants by using logic and persuasion. The top joint shows will power, decisiveness and a tendency to get one's way by decree rather than logic. Ideally, the top joint is slightly shorter than the middle joint and the whole thumb extends to the middle of the bottom joint of the index finger. The thumb should be supple but show a little resistance when you try to bend it backward. If you can collapse it with no effort, then the person is too easily swayed by other people's wishes. If it's rigid and tense, he is opinionated, autocratic and adapts poorly to change. You cannot test your own thumb and finger tension because you and your hands are too closely related, but it's more fun to have someone else test them for you anyway.

"Murderer's" thumb

Thumbtips

Square, spatulate and conical thumbtips have the same significance as square (practical), spatulate (dynamic), and conical (sensitive) fingertips, except that the thumbtip is more significant since it characterizes the person's will and general attitude toward the world. A few thumbtip shapes do not appear as fingertip shapes, to wit: a broad, flat thumb shows a firm, careful disposition. This is often called the "murderer's thumb" but this is unfair. If combined with an excessively high Venus mount and a shattered or short heart-line, this firmness of will might turn to cruelty, but most people with murderer's thumbs wouldn't murder a fly. All the people with murderer's thumbs whom I have met have been kind and responsible citizens. A paddle-shaped thumb is a sign of extreme determination. What paddle-thumb wants, paddle-thumb gets. A thumb which is conical at the top and has a narrow second phalange (the waisted thumb) shows tact and a pleasant personality. Regardless of its shape, if the thumbtip is flat when viewed from the side, the person has difficulty completing what he starts.

Waisted thumb

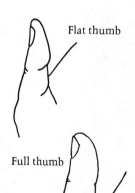

Flat thumb

Full thumb

The posture in which a person holds the thumb is also quite telling. Remember that the thumb represents the will, so its posture is a symbol of the person's overall mental state. Newborn babies keep their thumbs curled tight in their fists for the first few

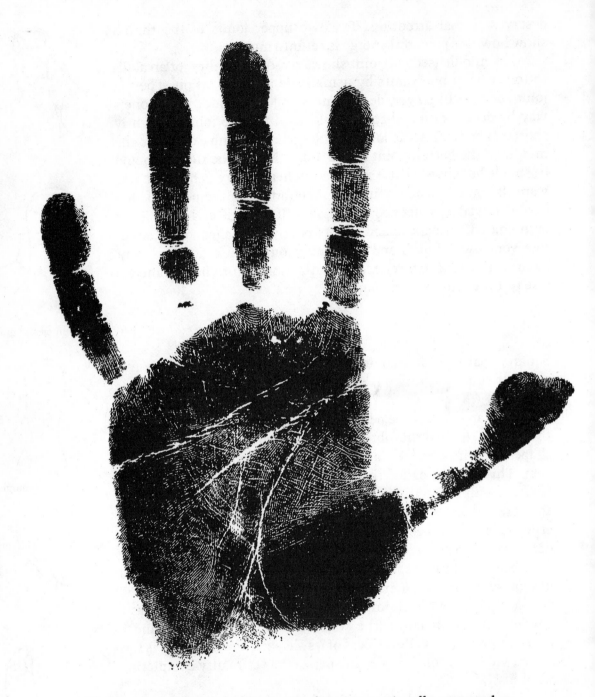

In the dominant left hand of James Sinclair, internationally respected financier, we see an outstanding combination of traits. His quadrants are well balanced, and he has a strong thumb and clear lines. These show that he has the strength, balance, and determination his job requires.

weeks of life. It's a sign that the child is accepting its transition to the nonuterine world when the thumb emerges from the little fist and begins to help the child grab the things it wants. When a child or adult returns the thumb to its hiding place in the fist, it shows that some anxiety or despair is too much to handle—it implies retreat. If the hands are clenched with the thumbs inside, it is a sign of powerful tension and anxiety. When the hands are folded with thumbs inside, read grief and black despair. On the contrary, if the thumb is held at a slight angle from the hand, the person has a spunky spirit and is happy to face life.

Now that you have the thumbshapes down pat, we'll review the meaning of the fingers.

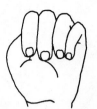

Clenched in palm

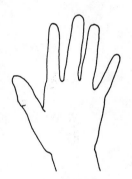

Bent over

Finger	Planet	Meaning
Index	Jupiter	*Self-confidence*, ambition, executive ability, money. Sometimes spiritual leadership.
Middle	Saturn	*Ideas of right and wrong*, search for truth, propriety, sometimes moralism or perfectionism.
Ring	Apollo	*Self-expression*, creativity, artistic interest and willingness to contact inner self.
Fifth	Mercury	*Verbal communication*, tact, willingness to relate, clarity or bluntness in speech.
Thumb	None	*Personal will*. Top joint shows will power, second joint shows reasoning.

Straight and firm

The clearer these basics become in your mind, the better you will be at palmreading.

Fingers Long and Short

Times change, lines change, mounts change, nearly everything changes. One thing that doesn't change, however, is the length of the fingers. (At least not unless you have an accident.) The finger

Flexed back

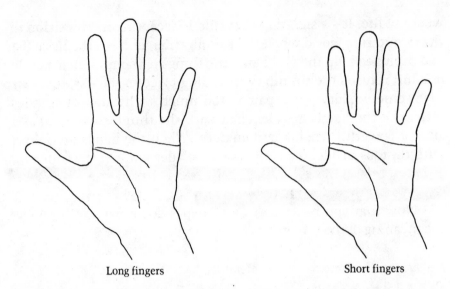

Long fingers   Short fingers

length tells you something about the person's basic temperament. Long fingers show a penchant for detailed work. People who have them tend to be nit-picky if allowed to run amok. Short fingers show that the person is geared more to the overall view. They are able to see the forest for the trees, and thus make better managers and organizers than their long-fingered friends. Each group can learn the tendencies of the other, so shorties can manage to balance their checkbooks and long-fingered folks can broaden their perspective, but their natural inclination will always follow the finger length.

More mathematically inclined palmists than myself have determined that if the Saturn finger extends three-fourths or more of the way down the palm when it is bent down toward the wrist, the fingers are long. If it goes little more than halfway down, they are short. My feeling is that if they look long, they are long and if they look short they are short, and most are normal.

If the fingers are naturally spaced wide apart, things tend to run easily through the person's hands, both literally and figuratively. People with hands like these spend money like water, often say too much and listen too little and generally have their stops opened up just one notch too wide. Keep checking them during the reading to make sure they still have their earphones on, otherwise you will have to repeat the whole thing. The positive side of having widely spaced fingers is that if the person can stay grounded and open at the same time, he is able to channel tremendous energy without depleting himself. Some great spiritual teachers have widely spaced fingers. Everything runs through them but they never run out.

Closely held fingers show a cautious nature, unwilling to part with money or information and likely to hold back when expressing feelings. When someone is feeling contracted because of temporary stress he may tighten or clench his hands, but when a guarded attitude becomes a way of life the fingers are always squeezed together. If both the fingers and the two hands are squashed together when the person presents his hands for inspection, it shows fear of change.

Once a man called and begged for a reading that same afternoon. He arrived precisely on time, wearing a tight-fitting green polyester business suit. He seemed uncomfortable at the prospect of visiting a palmist but desperate enough to try anything. In this case, I was anything. He held his small hands out, pressed so tightly together that I could barely pry them apart. His fingers were packed together like sardines. Every aspect of this man's bearing and demeanor backed up the information reflected in the posture of his hands. He had retreated from circumstances that were crushing him and he was too afraid to move. Many people are more willing to put up with unsatisfying jobs and marriages than they are to change, simply because they are afraid that things could be worse. To these people, the glass is not only half-empty—it has a leak! In addition to the other information that emerged from the reading, I recommended that he practice holding his hands in a more relaxed manner and allow the fingers to move a natural distance apart. Although changing the posture of the hands seems like a small thing, it eventually has a strong effect.

Hand Shapes

Just as there are different shapes of people, there are different shapes of hands. Several different ways of categorizing shapes of hands have been proposed through the centuries. The one most commonly used is that of Casimir Stanislas d'Arpentigny, a French palmist of the nineteenth century. We will use a variation of his system here.

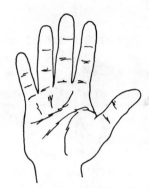

A square hand (earth)   A spatulate hand (fire)

D'Arpentigny proposed a classification of seven major hand types: Elementary, Square, Conic, Spatulate, Knotty, Psychic and Mixed. He included the mixed category because nearly everyone is in it. It is essential to remember in classifying shapes as well as every other aspect of the hands that there are no perfect types. Look for the dominant characteristics of the hand and don't worry about whether it is square with a little spatulate spice or some bizarre new hand shape. It is possible to be a little of both.

The system we will use combines d'Arpentigny's system with the four major elements of astrology. Thus, we have four major hand shapes: Square, Spatulate, Conic and Pointed. These correspond to the elements Earth, Fire, Water and Air, respectively. We eliminate d'Arpentigny's knotty hand because it is for arthritics as well as knotty thinkers. Elementary hands are a variation of square hands in which the fingers are stubbier and the lines coarser. The mixed category, as mentioned before, contains all of us, therefore it is not useful. What you want is to get a feeling for the hand. If you start to fret about whether your friend's hand is *really* square or spatulate, you've missed the point. For those of you who now realize you've missed it, the point is this:

Forget formalism.
Listen to the spirit of the person, not the categories of your mind.
Don't worry. Enjoy yourself.

Follow the Dotted Line

It is easiest to determine the hand shape by drawing an imaginary line around the palm, connecting the bottoms of all the fingers and excluding the thumb. Your line will run around the top of the

A conic hand (water)

A pointed hand (air)

palm, down the pinky side, around the wrist and straight up the thumb side of the hand without including the thumb in the outline. This should bring out a roughly square, spatulate, conical or pointed shape. If you connect the dots and discover the outline of a hippopotamus or a Soviet missile station, call me. I'll decide whether to call the CIA or the friendly doctors. Here they are, the four basic hands.

Square hands, associated with the element *Earth*, are of equal width at the base and beneath the fingers. They show a practical, rational nature. Square-handed people make good businessmen, and are competent and responsible. Their only weakness is a crying need to have a reason for everything. An elementary hand is better suited to simple labor.

Spatulate hands, associated with the element *Fire*, are narrower either at the base or near the fingers. They indicate a dynamic, independent nature. If the spatulate hand is broader at the base, the person is more active and will enjoy exotic activities like shooting the white water rapids in Brazil, while if the hand is broader up near the fingers, the love of adventure will focus on exploring unusual concepts, like palmistry or quantum physics.

Conic hands, associated with the element *Water*, are tapered slightly at the base and at the base of the fingers. People with conical hands adapt easily to the people and situations around them and often make better followers than leaders. They are helpful, intuitive souls.

Pointed hands, associated with the element *Air*, are long, thin and narrow. They look slightly neurasthenic, as though they

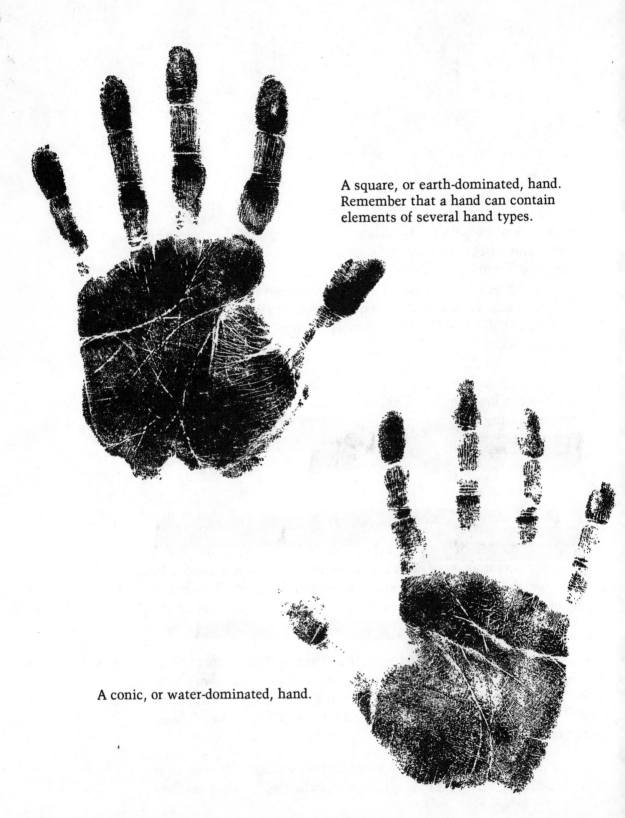

A square, or earth-dominated, hand. Remember that a hand can contain elements of several hand types.

A conic, or water-dominated, hand.

should be holding vials of smelling salts or be draped across Ophelia's lap. People with these hands are painfully sensitive and often idealistic. Since they are easily swayed by influences from their surroundings, they should make every effort to keep their environment peaceful.

The dominant element in a person's hands does not always correlate with the sun sign in the person's astrological chart. (The sun sign is the sign of the month you were born in.) However, the element of the hand is usually prominent in other aspects of the person's astrological chart. If you don't know anything about astrology, the foregoing explanation may be meaningless to you, but don't worry—even without a background in astrology, you can see that each of the four elements has certain characteristics, and that people you know seem to have these characteristics. Earth is heavy and dense, and so is the guy at the next desk. Water conforms to the shape of whatever form it's put in, and so does your sister-in-law. Fire is always roaming around once it gets out of hand, and so is—who? Air is light and spaced out, and so are a lot of people. Use your instinctive sense of the metaphorical meanings of the four elements to help you interpret the character through the shape of the hand.

Do Tip Your Hand

Fingertips have meaning too. Remember from the section on quadrants that the primary energies of the body and mind rise from the base of the palm and move into the active upper half of the hand. Heading northward up the hand, we see that the fingertips get the last clear shot at shaping the energy before it is extruded into the world. Thus, the shape of the fingertips tells you how the person shapes his power in the last flourish. There are four types of fingertips; most people have a combination of different types on their multifarious fingers. The basic shapes are: Square, Conical, Spatulate and Pointed.

Square fingertips show practicality, usefulness, balanced thought and a capacity for rational decisive action. They know how to fill out income tax forms and always have the plumber's phone number in their address book.

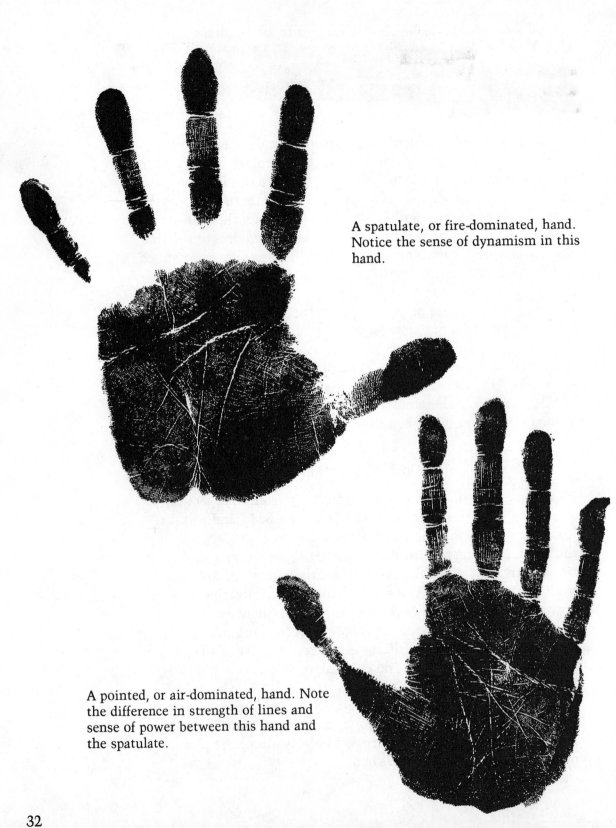

A spatulate, or fire-dominated, hand. Notice the sense of dynamism in this hand.

A pointed, or air-dominated, hand. Note the difference in strength of lines and sense of power between this hand and the spatulate.

Conical tips (slightly narrower at the top than at the base) indicate the same thing as conical hands—adaptability, sensitivity, appreciation of the arts, quick-wittedness and accurate intuition.

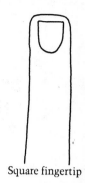

Square fingertip

Spatulate tips are slightly flared at the top. (These should be distinguished from clubbed fingertips, which look like cavemen's clubs and are either inherited or signify potential trouble in the cardiovascular system.) Spatulate tips indicate a creative flair for action, an impulsive and adventurous spirit, and an ability to instinctively arrange things and people into new and interesting combinations. Never try to stick a spatulate tip into a dull square hole.

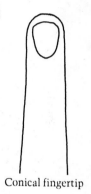

Conical fingertip

Pointed tips are the most idealistic and sensitive of all. They funnel energy smoothly in and out of the body, which means that their owners are easily overwhelmed by outside influences which their square tipped friends never perceive. People with pointed or conical hands and all pointed tips are likely to be too idealistic for life in the fast lane. In fact, they may have trouble getting on the freeway.

What you have just read was the tip types *out* of the context of an individual hand. In practice, bear in mind the type of hand on which the fingertips appear. Square fingertips on a pointed hand will show a conflict between the person's basic temperament and his natural style. The hand shape leads him to be soft and idealistic and the fingertips lead him to be hard-nosed. In case of conflicting messages from hand shape and tips, the hand shape has a more powerful determining effect on the character. Yet the tips, though not anonymous, still help you solve the case.

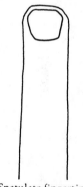

Spatulate fingertip

You now have a sense of the layout of the hands. You know the neighborhoods of Jupiter, Apollo, Saturn and Mercury. You know what to look for in the four quadrants and you know the difference between right and left. Classifying the hand shape lets you know whether you are dealing with someone ruled by fire, water, earth, or air. Please take a moment now and leaf back through this chapter. Find the various sections of your own hands and look at the information in the book again. It will sink in naturally as you read on, but feel familiar and comfortable with the material covered so far before moving on to the major landmarks and streets of the cities of your hands.

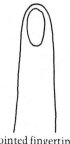

Pointed fingertip

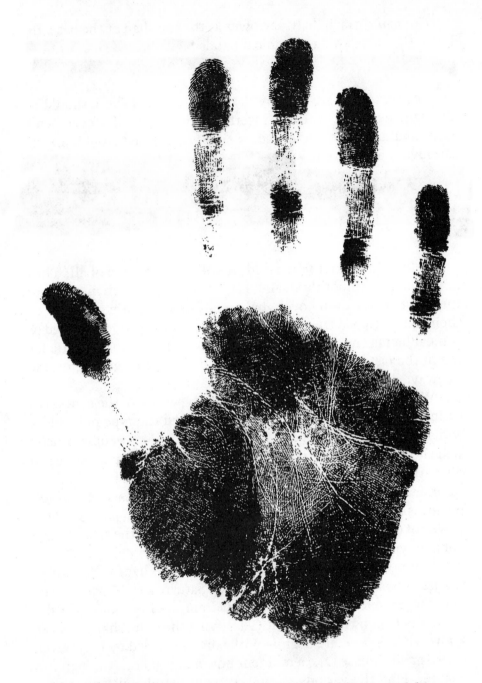

In the hand of television actress Lisa Marie, the lines are delicate, indicating that light, airy elements are strong in her hands. Her hand is slightly spatulate, showing that she also has a fiery side.

3

THE POWER
OF OBSERVATION

Sherlock Holmes once remarked, "You *see*, Watson, but you do not *observe*." He could have been speaking to us all. Conscious observation is one of our most potent tools, because observation leads to awareness and awareness leads to change. The subtlest signs in the hands can give you a wealth of information about an individual. Postures and gestures can tell you almost as much about the inner workings of a person's character as all the lines, mounts and marks put together. And you can learn a lot from those!

All of us have patterns of tension in our bodies and our minds—they show themselves in our behavior patterns such as compulsive eating or in physical patterns such as hunching the shoulders. Analogous patterns of tension appear in our hands. Noticing tension patterns is the first step toward breaking their grip on the personality. Watching changes in the patterns on the hands is a graphic way to monitor one's inner growth. Since the hands mirror all parts of life, they automatically reflect blocks in our energy or talent—sometimes in the lines and mounts but also in the posture.

Of course, tension is not all bad. It's one of the main things that distinguishes us from Jello pudding. When there's too much of it in the wrong places, however, it becomes a problem.

In this chapter we will talk more about *postures* than *gestures*. The difference between postures and gestures is in the amount of conscious will that is used to produce them. Gestures are deliberate, usually learned patterns of movement in the hand and arm which have a specific, often culturally defined meaning. They rarely last more than a few moments. Postures are chronic patterns of tension. People are rarely aware of their meaning, and, in fact, are frequently unaware of their existence. The posture of the hands in their "relaxed" state is a transparent indicator of the relative self-confidence, sense of morality, capacity for self-expression and communication, and will power of every individual. When you combine the meaning of the posture with the comparative meanings of the two hands (dominant relating to the externalized personality and nondominant relating to the world within), you can see the subtlest details of a person's psychology.

For example, I once did a palmreading for a woman who is the translator for a foreign dignitary. On her dominant right hand, the Mercury finger was strong, supple and perfectly straight. Recalling that Mercury rules communication, this tells us that in her dealings with the public, she communicated clearly and directly. However, the Mercury finger on her left hand was bent nearly in half. Thus, although she communicated very clearly to the thousands of people who heard her translate for her employer, she was still shy in presenting her own thoughts. That slight blockage in communicating about her inner self was shown by the disproportionate tension in the "communication finger" of her nondominant hand. Sometimes you can feel these patterns by flexing each finger back and forth and feeling how tense or relaxed it is. However, the tension patterns frequently show up in the physical carriage of the fingers and hands.

Glance discreetly at the hands of the next person you see. Are all of the fingers relaxed and extended naturally with Jupiter and Saturn nearly straight and Apollo and Mercury slightly curved? Is the thumb held at a natural distance from the palm, neither swaybacked nor huddled down into the hand? Any variations from this pattern have specific meanings which you will learn to deduce for yourself by using your power of observation, your psychic sense, and your knowledge of what each part of the hand means.

Natural hand posture

Five Little Fingers and What They Knew

As previously explained, each finger has a specific meaning associated with the attributes of a certain god. The thumb represents the personal will. The Jupiter, or index finger, represents self-confidence, leadership and executive ability. Saturn, the middle finger, represents morality, self-criticism and a sense of propriety or right and wrong; it also represents introspection and the search for truth. The ring finger, Apollo, shows self-expression and creativity, and is the first finger on the inner-oriented side of the hand. At the end of the track comes the Mercury finger. Mercury rules communication and verbal expression; therefore it also indicates clarity in relationships.

The moment you feel blocked in one of these areas of your personality, tension appears in the corresponding finger. Suppose that what you really want to do is fly a kite. You are about to walk out the door, kite in hand, when the phone rings. It's your mother, reminding you that you are late for her Mahjong party. Down tumbles the kite and you are off to unwillingly fulfill your filial duty. How would this plight appear on your hands? When you are doing exactly what you want to do, your thumbs are relaxed because your will is relaxed. Since your inner desires match your outer behavior, there is little difference in the tension level of the two thumbs. The instant your behavior diverges from your true will, conflict begins, and from that springs tension. You might pretend that everything is fine and thus keep your dominant thumb relaxed, but the wrenchings of your inner mind will assert themselves somewhere. The tension materializes on your nondominant hand.

The signs of inner tension are sometimes subtle, taking the forms of raised blood pressure, changes in certain hormonal levels or gradual buildups of muscular tension. Although these signs are hard to spot in the beginning, they can develop into serious diseases and psychological disorders if their cause is not recognized and eliminated. These signs of inner tension, which may be hard to feel in the whole body, are easily seen on the hands. When you tense up, your thumbs tense up. If you stubbornly resist acting against your will, the tension will be greater in your dominant thumb. In such a case the tension is right out there where you can see it. If, however, you submerge your resistance and persist in doing what you do not want to do, then the tension will show up in your nondominant thumb, that is, on the side that reflects the parts of yourself you would rather hide from the world. By seeing and feeling the tension in your thumbs you can gauge your inner and outer-directed tensions.

In the case of the Mahjong party, the tension in your nondominant thumb will last as long as the dice are hitting the board. The moment your kitetails hit the sky, your thumbs will relax. If you habitually do what you don't want to do, hedging about your true wishes and not acknowledging your self-suppression, this tension pattern will become a regular part of your life. That thumb will stay tense or clutched to the palm, reinforcing your sense of acting against your true will. By becoming aware of this pattern in your behavior and by massaging away the tension in your nondominant thumb, you begin to free yourself of unnecessary limitation.

When you first examine someone's palms, it might be difficult to tell whether their postures are chronic or temporary. If they are temporary, they don't require a long discussion. Perhaps that nondominant thumb is tense because the person doesn't really want her hands read! Hold the hands quietly and keep looking at them for several minutes. As the person relaxes, temporary postures will fade and chronic ones will remain.

Persnickety Patterns

Although any finger on either hand can become a reservoir of tension, certain syndromes appear regularly. You could deduce all of these for yourself, but we will cover the ones you are most likely to encounter. They are:

- The Businessperson's Syndrome
- The Non-Socratic Syndrome
- The Milquetoast Syndrome
- The Hidden Critic's Syndrome
- The Pseudocommunicator's Syndrome
- The Withholder's Syndrome

The Businessperson's Syndrome

This syndrome is commonly found among men and women who focus primarily on the world outside themselves—business, politics, social status, and so forth. Absorbed in playing a game in which nobody wins points for being happy, they lose touch with their inner selves. They get out of the habit of saying what they really mean. In the end they forget that they are human beings enlivened by Divine Love, and come to believe that they are their job, or their club membership, or whatever it is that they focus on outside themselves. Cut off from their inner sources of inspiration, they seek in ever widening circles the satisfaction they lack within. Actually, they do not lack it—it is waiting patiently inside them, unnoticed. They are not looking at it.

The Businessperson's Syndrome. The Non-Socratic Syndrome looks the same but appears on the nondominant hand.

The Businessperson's Syndrome is composed of bent Apollo and Mercury fingers on the dominant hand. Apollo and Mercury are on the inner-oriented side of the hand, channelling the energy of self-expression, intuition and verbal communication out into the world. When these fingers are habitually curled, it is a sign that their energies are being blocked. The Businessperson's Syndrome arises initially when the individual shuts down her connection to her inner self, often telling herself things like, "I'd better keep my mouth shut," or "If he knew how I felt, he'd kill me." The posture can also come from an unwillingness to face some truth or unacknowledged fear that is hovering inside. Once established, this posture becomes an unconscious habit and reinforces the pattern of energy blockage.

Once an individual knows how she is holding her hands and what her posture means, she can begin to change the patterns simply by straightening those two fingers. Just as she created her current pattern of blockage and unconsciousness, she can create a new habit of openness and awareness by gently massaging the Apollo and Mercury fingers, straightening and bending them slightly backward with each massage. The physical movement alone begins to release some of the inner-directed energy so that the person can regain contact with her inner feelings.

The Non-Socratic Syndrome

The Non-Socratic Syndrome is so named because the people who have it do not know themselves. Whereas in the Businessperson's Syndrome the Apollo and Mercury fingers are bent on the dominant hand, Non-Socratics have these same fingers bent on the non-dominant hand. This is paradoxical, since the nondominant hand represents the inner self and so do the Apollo and Mercury fingers. Having Apollo and Mercury bent on the inner-oriented hand shows that the person is out of touch with himself at a deep inner level. This sounds like quite a trick, but a lot of people manage to do it.

When a person loses touch with her inner self, she loses touch with her power source. She tries to live off surface energy alone, expanding endlessly into the world without a firm foundation. Dealing with these people is like getting the bun without the hamburger. They have a smooth surface but provide no nutritional value. It's as though they want to run their cars on the gas in the engine without ever drawing from the gas tank. Although deeply out of touch with their sources of self-expression and communication—as shown by the blockage in the inner-oriented fingers of the nondominant hand—Non-Socratic people try to keep up appearances, giving the impression (probably a very convincing one) that they are in touch with their inner feelings and are willing to communicate freely. This is not true, and although everyone else might fall for the act, at least one person knows that her semblance of self-knowledge is groundless, and that is the person who's putting on the act. From her constant insincerity grows a malaise which begins to permeate her life and leads her even more deeply into self-distrust. If she returns to her internal energy and to a willingness to share herself with the world, the tinny ring of her experience will be replaced by a rich, melodious sound.

Non-Socratics do not develop this syndrome because they are bad, covert people, they do it because they are afraid. At some point, they decided that the safest self-expression was no self-expression at all, and they have lived their lives out of this decision. The more love you can provide, the easier it will be for these people to trust their own feelings when you are around. With awareness and practice, they can rewrite the script of their lives and, if they so choose, return to the pleasure of knowing themselves. A very practical place to begin dealing with this pattern is in the hands. Massage the nondominant Apollo and Mercury fingers gently, straightening them and flexing them slightly backward.

The Milquetoast Syndrome

The Milquetoast Syndrome, so called because it appears on the hands of the meek, is a strong difference in the tension level of the thumbs. When the dominant thumb is relaxed and flexible and the nondominant thumb is rigid, you know that the individual is hiding inner tension. The nondominant hand shows the inner life. The Milquetoast Syndrome often appears in the hands of frustrated people because they are claiming that everything is fine when it is not. The dominant thumb is flexible, indicating that they are manifesting relaxation and adaptability, but the nondominant thumb is extremely tense, showing their true will is being suppressed. Since their happiness is held together by self-suppression rather than self-actualization, they have to work at it constantly. In my book, working at being happy is about the same as being unhappy. Milquetoast people often give the impression that they have everything they want. They are big on saying, "Whatever you want, dear," and "Whatever you think, boss." All the time they are saying this, tension is building inside.

Dominant

Beware of people who never assert their will. Nobody is that much of a non-entity. People with the Milquetoast Syndrome often have an unexamined fear that something devastating will happen if they do what they really want to do (their loved ones might leave them, the sky might fall, etc.) but in fact, something devastating will happen if they don't. Our true will does manifest itself one way or another, so we might as well let it do us good. It is one of our strongest creative powers. So whenever you see a rigid nondominant thumb, for heaven's sake, massage it!

Non-dominant

Of course there are moments in all of our lives when we must do things we don't want to do—attend boring parties or lectures, wait in line at the Post Office—a thousand things require us to adapt our immediate desires to the requirements of the moment. At all these times our nondominant thumb is likely to tense up. This slight tension is part of everyday life and is not a problem, since we relax as soon as the tension is past. The Milquetoast Syndrome is chronic.

When you notice the Milquetoast pattern, realize that the person is probably in a life situation—marriage, family or job, which supports her in repressing herself. Her spouse or employer is getting benefits from domineering, and the person herself is getting benefits out of staying in the comfort zone of not taking responsibility for her own desires. She is likely to consider other people responsible for her predicament (mistake number one). Because of all of this, she won't take very kindly to being told that she lies about what she wants all the time. Be tactful and don't attack the problem head on. The root of this syndrome is the person's lack of faith in her own intrinsic value, so by supporting her in the belief that she does have value and that her desires are worthwhile, you assist her in breaking her pattern.

The Hidden
Critic's Syndrome

Dominant

Nondominant

The Hidden Critic's Syndrome

The Milquetoast Syndrome is unhealthy for the person who has it, but the Hidden Critic's Syndrome is unhealthy both for the person who has it and her friends. It appears as a discrepancy between the tension levels of the Saturn fingers. Saturn represents self-criticism and ideas of right and wrong. While it is great to have a sense of ethics, it is also possible to have too much of a good thing. In this syndrome, the Saturn finger on the dominant hand is relaxed and supple, indicating open-minded moral views without inordinate self-criticism. So far, so good. It is on the other hand that trouble crops up. The nondominant Saturn finger is rigid, and sometimes it even juts out stiffly from the hand. This reveals that the person is far more critical than she admits. She is likely to lead friends and lovers into unsuspected traps by acting incredibly tolerant while she keeps score of their sins inside. She seems so non-judgmental that they blithely do what they like. Then they transgress her hidden but powerful moral code and blammo! She either blows up, freezes up, or worst of all, she shows no response at all but holds it against them for the rest of her life.

Encourage people with this pattern of tension to become more conscious of their need to criticize themselves and others, and to see how it interferes with their feelings of spontaneous love. Moral standards are valuable, but not when they sabotage the inner spirit. When people experience the Conscious Love within themselves, they don't need oppressive dogmas. Once again, un-awareness of one's inner magnificence leads one to pain. Gently remind the Hidden Critic that an excessive need to criticize others usually springs from dislike of oneself. Whatever we resist most in ourselves will turn up continually in the people we meet. When she sees that her over-moralism stems more from her need to criticize than from the other person's wrongness, her grousing will stop. She can also massage the nondominant Saturn finger to free some of the blocked energy there and feel more internal freedom. Finally, if she must have such rigid rules about what's right and wrong, beg her to tell everybody else her rules. Then, at least, they will know whether they want to play.

Communication Blocks: Pseudocommunicators and Withholders

The last two syndromes in this chapter concern communication. They are the Pseudocommunicator's Syndrome and the Withholder's Syndrome. A pseudocommunicator is someone who pretends to communicate openly when in fact she is not saying anything at all, and a withholder is someone who knows what she wants to say and doesn't say it. Pseudocommunicators usually have little intention to communicate. Their barrage of words acts more as a barrier against communication than as a channel for it. Withholders try to say it all with silence. They don't usually have much luck.

Pseudo-communicator's Syndrome

You can spot the cagey Pseudocommunicator by her bent Apollo finger and her straight, firm Mercury finger. Apollo rules self-expression and Mercury rules communication, particularly verbal skills. These two areas are inherently related, since self-expression is actually the content of communication. Without the sincere expression of meaning which is contributed by the energy of Apollo, Mercury's glib tongue just fans the air. The bent Apollo finger shows an unwillingness to bare one's true feelings. The straight Mercury finger, which is sometimes so gorged with energy that it juts out slightly from the palm, shows that great effort is put into verbal expression. This means that a lot of talking is going on, but very little is being said. The person can remedy this by massaging both Mercury fingers and by listening to herself talk.

By listening to herself as she talks, she will come to see how little she usually says.

When both Apollo and Mercury are straight, the individual is deeply expressive and in touch with her inner nature. When both of them are bent, as in the Businessperson's Syndrome, it shows a general unwillingness to either know *or* express her true self. However, when your friend with Apollo bent and Mercury standing at attention calls you up, you will know that you can put the phone receiver on the table, clean the kitchen, balance your checkbook, and get something to drink, and when you pick up the phone again and say "Uh huh?" to your rambling friend, you won't have missed a thing.

Withholder's Syndrome

Dominant

Nondominant

The Cost of Withholding

When the Mercury finger on the dominant hand is bent down and the Mercury finger on the nondominant hand is straight, you have a Withholder in hand. The disparity between the sides shows that while the desire to communicate is internally strong, it is being blocked. The mind is active, but nothing is coming out of the mouth except perhaps a gentle sigh. All of us withhold at times, because it is not always appropriate to speak our minds. Our focus here is on chronic patterns rather than temporary situations. True Withholders compose long speeches in their minds—and leave them there. They know exactly what they want to say, as shown by the strength of the nondominant Mercury finger, but they never say it.

One of my clients is a South American woman who was raised to believe that she ought never reveal her true feelings to anyone outside the family. There were even limitations on communication within the family based on seniority and etiquette. Her hands formed a classic Withholder's Syndrome, with Mercury bent on the dominant side and straight as a soldier on the nondominant side. Nevertheless, blocked communication was not her complaint. (Withholders rarely think they have a problem with communication. Since they don't do it, the issue does not arise.) No, her complaint was that she couldn't find anyone worth communicating with. Everyone she knew was so shallow and superficial, she said, that she didn't feel comfortable opening up to them. She felt alienated and alone among her best friends.

This feeling of aloneness is one of the most unfortunate by-products of withholding communication. Withholders do not share themselves with others, so others have no way of knowing who the Withholder really is. Then the Withholder feels unknown and unloved even by those who claim to know her best, and she withdraws further into her alienation. Her companions notice, consciously, or unconsciously, that she never reveals her true feelings, and conclude, consciously, or unconsciously, that if she's on guard maybe they had better be on guard too. They in turn withhold, and the cycle is perpetuated. Everyone involved is left with the frustrating sensation of being weighted down by misunderstanding and undelivered communications.

Chronically withholding communication is like always inhaling without exhaling, or like eating without ever excreting. It can make you sick. The following quotation has been a great inspiration to me and to my clients in opening up to greater communication. It was written by Jeff Linzer, about whom I know nothing except that he wrote this:

Love

Others will never be able to love you as you want to be loved until you are willing to communicate yourself to them completely—getting them to understand your barriers (what stands between you and them), your fears (what you think will be the consequences of your honesty: rejection, loneliness, ridicule, torture, death . . .). Through slowly developing the confidence that others can accept and understand you, you can begin to present yourself to them as you really are, without disguises. You can tell them more of what you really think about things, more about what you want from them, what you're like, what you feel. As you learn to trust your ability to get yourself across to those closest to you, you realize that you have the ability to present yourself to anyone you wish.

Games have nothing to do with love, except to demonstrate that you are afraid of losing something, of being hurt and betrayed. But you cannot lose in love, because love is not a game.

Let it happen. Love will be there when you stop trying to create an effect. Letting go of your ego means only that you stop caring what you think the other thinks of you, and just relate to him as you know you are. Let it happen. You'll be loved by everyone when you decide to love all of them, when you commit yourself to fulfilling your end of your love affair with all others. Open your heart and mind to the infinite excitement of your relationship to every living being. You'll discover that you and everyone else would give anything to experience the pure love that relates us all. And the only thing there is to give is yourself.

Encourage both Pseudocommunicators and Withholders to take a chance on communication—it might not bite after all. Suggest they make a habit of massaging the Apollo and Mercury fingers to help them re-establish contact with their inner selves and love themselves as they are.

Make Your Own Patterns

The patterns we have covered so far are only a few of the infinite variety of postures that the hands can take. You might see classic examples of self-suppression, hidden criticism, or withheld communication along with countless variations on each theme. Use your knowledge of the meaning of each finger and your careful observation of the hands to help you form conclusions. Is the Jupiter finger always held over Saturn? Then personal ambition overpowers the sense of morality. Does the Saturn finger partially obscure Apollo? Then the sense of propriety is squelching art and self-expression. Each person has her own postural variations just as each person has her unique life. When you see these patterns in yourself, remember what they mean. When you see them in your friends, lightly point them out and let them decide what they choose to do with the information.

Unless we are aware of our behavior patterns and barriers, they become so much a part of us that we don't know they are there. They move when we move, and whenever we try to catch a glimpse of them they vanish into the woodwork. Thus, anything we do which increases our awareness of the beliefs, attitudes and fears which run our lives is helpful. We needn't fight our fears, because fighting them makes them stronger. If we look at them calmly they will spontaneously disappear.

Watching the postures of the hands is one way to become more aware of our thoughts, beliefs and changing feelings. If you have a chronic tension pattern in your hands, be conscious of it as often as possible. If you know someone who has a pattern, point it out. Remember what the pattern means, and make a habit of massaging the finger or fingers that form the unnatural pose. Balance the energy and release the tensions in the microcosm of your hand and stay gently, objectively aware of your posture and your behavior. Observation leads to awareness. Awareness leads to transformation. And transformation is the realization that your original nature is Love.

4

LINEUP ON THE HANDS

Lines are the streets in the cities of the hands: they transport energy from one part of the hand to another. Like streets, they have two major functions. They carry traffic and they are landmarks. Each line carries a specific type of energy. There are four major lines: the Life Line, the Heart Line, the Head Line, and the Fate Line. The life line reveals general vitality and records events of everyday life, the heart line reflects emotional attitudes, and the head line shows how rationally or imaginatively the person thinks. The fate line is also considered a major line because most people have it. There are also secondary lines and "lines of influence" which transport particular types of energy from one part of the hand to another. For example, a line of influence connecting the lines of head and heart shows a strong relationship between the emotions and the intellect. Although the line itself has no name, its function is clear because of its location. It blends the energy of the two major lines. All lines have one thing in common: they are rivers of energy.

If you drive into a city and find the streets rutted with cracks and potholes, you'll suppose that the city is poorly kept up. In the same way, the condition of the lines shows you the condition of the person's energy. Clear, deep lines show strong, stable energy,

48

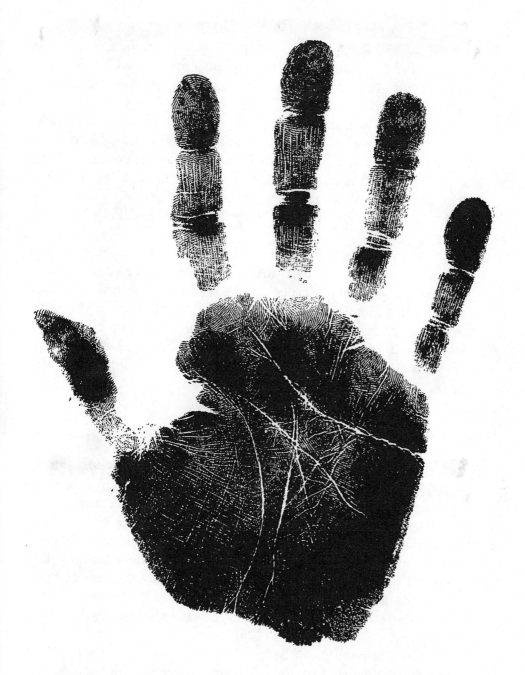

The hand of well-known actress Eileen Brennan is strong, yet the lines are fine. This shows that she has both the stability and the sensitivity to be a successful actress.

divided lines show divided energy, diffused lines show diffused energy, and so forth. It is rare to find someone in whom every line is clear and deep, just as it's rare to find a town in which no roads need repair. Fortunately, it is just as unusual to find hands in which all the lines are feeble.

There are four main lines and five minor lines on the hands. Most people have two or three of the main lines, and may not have any minor ones at all. The only line you really cannot do without is the life line. It is like the spinal cord of the hand. It is possible to lack one of the other major lines, but as far as I know, no one lacks them all. (If everybody didn't have them, they wouldn't be major lines.)

The minor lines are less common and less important. If the major lines are weak, then minor lines, no matter how valiant, will not help. (This is especially so when the life line is weak.) Minor lines augment the energy of the major lines in the same way that accessories accent an outfit. The right scarf can make a so-so outfit great, but it cannot turn a rag into a Halston. Major lines have a more compelling influence on the life than minor ones.

Meet Me On Main Street

The Life Line is the central line of the hand. All major events of the life are recorded on it. It also reflects the level of physical vitality, the attitude toward travel and adventure, and in certain cases, the length of the life. People are often obsessed with the length of their life line as if their days were measured by this groove on their hands, but this is a grievous mistake. Longevity depends on will to live and destiny, and the life line does not always reflect both. Thus, you might meet someone with a short life line and a strong will to live who is living far beyond the age indicated by the length of the line.

It is also possible to have a long life line and a short life. A Hungarian physician told me of several cases in which destiny interrupted the natural span of a person's life. This doctor was a battlefield medic during World War II. Having learned palmistry from her gypsy mother as a child, she examined the soldiers' palms as well as their pulses. She found that many of the fallen men had life

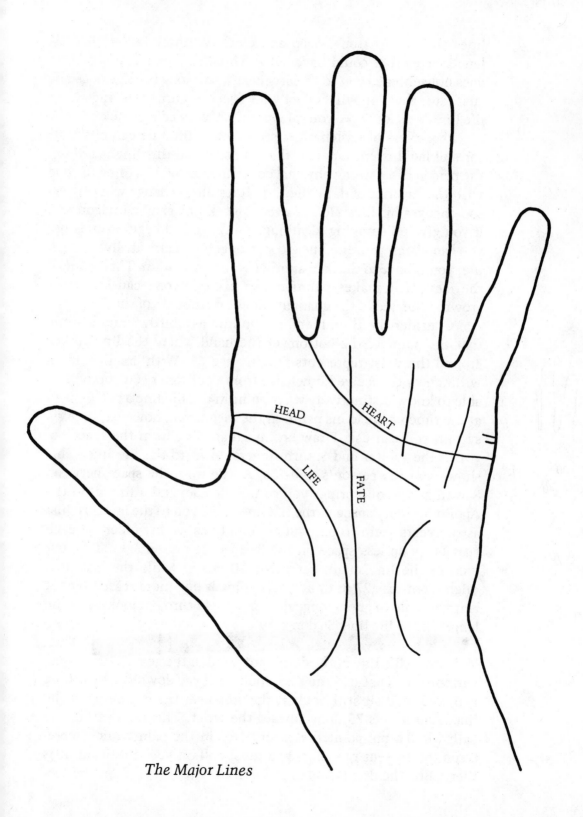

The Major Lines

lines that were strong, deep and clear. Whining bullets had silenced lives that could have sung. Thus, just as a short life line does not sentence you to an early death, so a long life line does not guarantee that you will collect your Social Security. Having a long life line does not make you safe in front of a speeding truck.

Regardless of its length, a strong clear life line can offset all sorts of lackluster marks on the hands. When this line is strong, the person has a strong physical constitution and is willing to cope with the vagaries of daily life. Life lines often change when a person changes his lifestyle and even a weak line can be invigorated. If you give up smoking, drinking and drugs and begin exercising, you can watch your life line grow strong. If you already live a clean life, you'll have to think of another way to beef it up. This is one of the facts that makes palmistry so exciting: one can see inner growth reflected in the changing lines and mounts of the palms.

Consider the thumb end of the line as "birth," and assume that the point at the bottom of the hand where the line curves around the wrist represents roughly age 65. With practice and a willingness to receive knowledge from your inner self you will be able to know instinctively what point in the life line a person is in at the time you read his palm. In the meantime, however, here's a system you can use. Draw an imaginary line from the space between the Jupiter and Saturn fingers down to the life line. This shows you the person's mid-20s. A line from the space between Saturn and Apollo brings you to middle age, and a line from the Apollo-Mercury space to the life line takes you to the late 50s. Just as the years seem to pass more quickly as we get older, so each year takes up less space on the line as the person ages. The first inch of the line might represent 20 years, while the last inch might comprise 27 or more years. This is one more reason why it is impossible to guess longevity accurately through looking at the length of the life line. So don't try.

Before you read a person's palms, ask him how old he is. Then look at the life line of the dominant hand in the general area of his current age. That is, if he's 35, look half-way down the line. If he is 5, and he'll sit still, look at the area near the beginning of the line. And if he's 75, look toward the wrist. This puts you in the ballpark. To pin-point the exact place in the palm which represents the present moment, you must call on your intuition. It is there. Breathe deeply, relax and don't try too hard. Scan the sec-

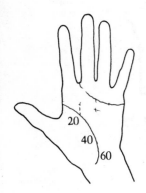

Measuring age on the life line

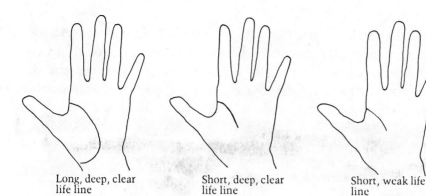

Long, deep, clear life line — Short, deep, clear life line — Short, weak life line — Life line ends on Luna

tion of the life line that comes closest to his age. Mentally ask, "Where is he on this line now?" and trust the inner response. With practice you will be able to go directly to the appropriate spot on the line.

Here are the major variations of the *life line:*

Appearance	Meaning
Long, deep, clear	Excellent vitality, minimal heartache, grounded in the physical world and able to cope with everyday life.
Short, deep, clear	Intense, somewhat reckless. Tends to rocket through activities and burn out early.
Short, weak	Perpetually blasé, uninterested in the world outside himself, often frail or sickly.
Ending on the Mount of Luna	Adventurous spirit, love of travel, may settle in a foreign country.
Arches toward the Mount of Luna then returns to curve around the thumb.	Travels extensively, explores new frontiers and eventually returns home.
Connected to the head line	Conservative and cautious due to strong early attachment to family. The longer these two lines are connected, the longer the person is enfolded in the family.
Splits in two halfway down the palm	Grows more adventurous as time goes by.

Life line arching to Luna, ending on Venus

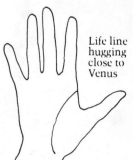

Life line hugging close to Venus

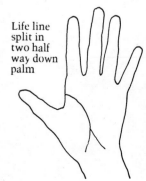

Life line split in two half way down palm

The condition of the life line sets the tone for the rest of the hand. Examine it carefully, for you will refer back to it throughout the reading. Also be sure to notice any differences between the life lines of the right and left hands, as these tell you the difference between the person's potential and what he's doing with it. If the line is strong on the nondominant side and weak on the dominant side, you know that he has blocks against using his full vitality. If the line is deeper on the dominant side, you know he is getting maximum mileage from the energy at hand. The life line records all major cycles and events of the life and indicates the person's willingness to relate to the physical world.

A weak life line. Notice that this line is particularly weak during the middle years.

A strong life line. Lucky man!

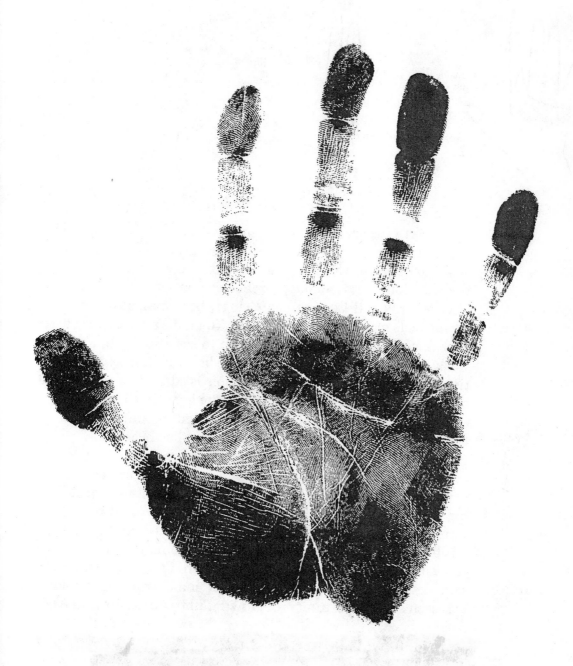

In the hand of popular singer Kenny Rankin, we see that the life line becomes much stronger in midlfe. This shows that he truly has a better second half.

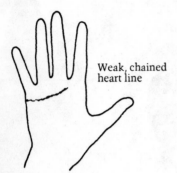

Weak, chained heart line

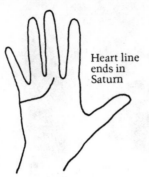

Heart line ends in Saturn

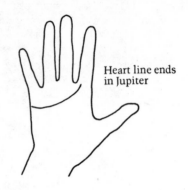

Heart line ends in Jupiter

The Heart Line

The Heart Line speaks of love. Since it relates to the subject closest to people's hearts, give it special attention. The heart line reveals attitudes toward love and records the emotional history of the individual. Its condition reflects emotional constancy and strength. Like all lines, it can change, becoming stronger as the person feels more confidence in love. You are far more likely to see a weak heart line become strong than to see a strong line become weak. The form of the line reveals the basic attitudes toward relationships, that is, whether the person is idealistic, unattached, balanced or not interested. Marks on the heart line have the same significance as on other lines: they represent modifications of the energy, in this case, the emotional energy. The heart line does not relate to marriage per se; marriages appear on the marriage lines.

When interpreting the heart line, accentuate the positive. Experiences which seem devastating in the moment may have healing effects over time. Emotional "bad habits" can also be transformed into qualities that increase love. Perfectionism can turn to an ability to see perfection in everyone. Chronic mistrust can turn to cautious but forgiving awareness. Even a tragic romance contains lessons that strengthen character and deepen compassion if it is seen as an opportunity for growth rather than a pie in the face from fate.

A deep, clear heart line shows a steadfast heart, and a chained heart line shows a history of disappointment in love. Chained heart lines are more common than chain letters, and they're about as profitable. When the line is chained, we hesitate to trust, and may not accept love when it is offered. People with chained heart lines are often full of love, they only need the opportunity and the courage to show it. Chain-lined peoples' feeling that love is scarce

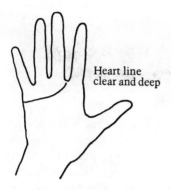

Heart line
clear and deep

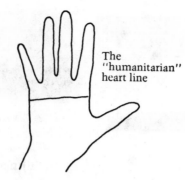

The
"humanitarian"
heart line

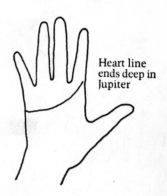

Heart line
ends deep in
Jupiter

and comes not from a true scarcity but from beliefs about love. Since the chains are in our own minds, we ourselves can dissolve them and return to the love that is our foundation. This is why a chained heart line can actually be a boon. The discomfort it represents spurs us on to find the unconditional love which illuminates all.

The end of the heart line closer to Jupiter relates attitudes about relationships. Here are the variations in the endings of the *heart line:*

Appearance	*Meaning*
Ending deep in the Mount of Saturn	Idealism and perfectionism in relationships. Sometimes this turns to ruthless self-criticism as the person demands from himself the perfection he cannot find in others.
Ending in the Mount of Jupiter	Passion in love combined with self-centeredness.
Ending deep in the Mount of Jupiter (almost running off the hand)	Spiritual love. Love of God greater than love of man. This line is rare, but not everyone who has it appreciates it. (I once taught a seminar on compatibility at a singles' club. There I met one of the few people I've seen who has a heart line ending so deeply in Jupiter. She smiled when I congratulated her on her great capacity for spiritual love and said, ''I know that's my inclination, but I don't like it. All I want is a boyfriend.'' You can't win with some people.)

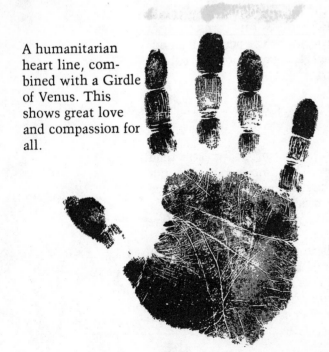

Heart line ends
halfway

Ending just between the Mount of Jupiter and the Mount of Saturn	Realistic, mature attitude about relationships. Knows what to reasonably expect from relationships and accepts people as they are. Loves to give and receive affection.
Crossing the entire palm	The "humanitarian" heart line. Shows universal love, a willingness to be involved with humanity in general and an unwillingness to get deeply attached to one particular person. Cannot comprehend possessiveness.
Ending halfway across the hand	Needs distance in relationships, tends to keep people at arm's length. A deep short line says he's very loving—up to a point. Don't press beyond that point and you'll be happy together. A chained, short line says he's so gun-shy about involvement that even a little smooch might activate his defenses.

Everyone has the capacity to love. The heart line only shows the form that love is most likely to take.

A humanitarian heart line, combined with a Girdle of Venus. This shows great love and compassion for all.

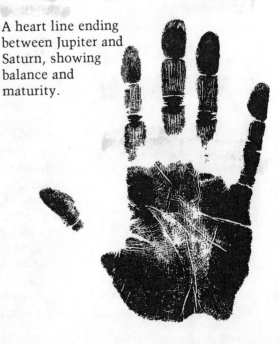

A heart line ending between Jupiter and Saturn, showing balance and maturity.

News About Head Lines

The Head Line reflects the mind. Its shape, straight or curved, tells the mode in which the person usually thinks—analytically, imaginatively or nuttily. In general, a straight head line shows rational thinking and a curved head line shows an imaginative bent. The line's condition, that is, its depth and clarity or lack of same, shows you whether his thoughts are razor sharp or marshmallow soft. The color of the line can also be significant. Mental problems such as chronic depression create a dark color tone in the whole line, and recurrent depressions appear as a series of dark dots on the line.

Long head line

The head line on the dominant hand often differs markedly from its counterpart on the other hand. This difference indicates the way in which the person has adapted his native mind to the rules of the "real world." A curved, or imaginative head line on the nondominant hand might become a ramrod rational line on the dominant hand, showing that although his natural inclination is toward the creative, he has taught himself to favor analysis. This is what happens when potential poets become CPAs instead.

Here are the major variations of the *head line:*

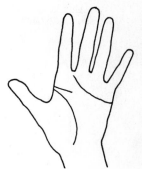

Short head line

Shape	Meaning
Runs straight more than halfway across the hand	Strong analytical intelligence and rational mind.
Runs straight less than halfway across the hand	Analytical mind tending to single-mindedness. If he likes engineering, that's all he talks about. ("Beautiful engineering today, huh?" "Let's go engineering, darling . . .")
Forks into sections, one straight and one sloped downward	Balanced judgement, always sees both sides of issues. Able to use both reason and imagination as appropriate. Trust this person to settle disputes fairly.
Bends slightly toward Luna	Clever, versatile imagination, still based in the rational mind.

Forked head line

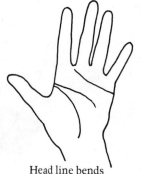

Head line bends slightly to Luna

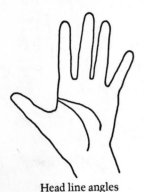

Head line angles sharply to Luna

Angles sharply toward Luna.

Irrepressible imagination. Great for creativity, tough for reality. These people may suffer from anxiety or delusions if they do not learn to control their fantasies.

Angles down and exactly parallels the life line.

Highly creative and productive artistic talent. This form usually appears in creative writers or composers. When the head line parallels the life line the two energies resonate and turn imagination into concrete reality.

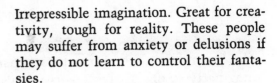

Head line cutting across hand (Sydney line).

Cuts completely across the hand. (This is also called the Sydney line, because it was first described in that city.)

Extreme, almost excessive insight. When a horizontal line cuts the hand in two, energy flow between the two halves of the hand is disrupted.

A line extending most of the way across the hand shows insight and diverse intellectual interests. When it cuts the hand in half the person becomes bitingly analytical and insightful, often to his own dismay. He knows too much.

Medical research on people with Sydney lines shows that they are more likely to have behaviorial problems such as hyperactivity or speech and hearing problems when they are young.

A straight, clear head line.

In the well-balanced hand of Bob Dolce, we see a headline curving toward Luna.

The *condition* of the head line is also significant, to wit:

Condition	Meaning
Clear and deep	A clear thinker. If the line is straight and clear, the person reaches rational conclusions smoothly. If a clear headline is curved, the person taps his creativity with ease, yea, panache.
Chained	Confused. Has difficulty defining problems and coming to practical solutions. People with these lines often benefit by eliminating sugar from their diets and getting more exercise; this maximizes whatever potential for mental clarity they have. Otherwise they could consider buying a guide dog.
Wavering	Draws conclusions in a roundabout way. Goes from Los Angeles to New York via Tokyo.

Wavering
head line

When interpreting the hands, use the information from the head line to help you communicate effectively. If the line is deep and straight, get straight to the point. He can take it. If it's frail and curved, be gentler. Use plenty of examples and metaphors to get your point across. The roundabout approach might drive a straight-lined person nuts, but it's the best way to get through to a more vulnerable mind. When reading head lines, remember that a straight line shows rational thinking and a curved line shows imagination. A deep line shows a clear mind and a faint line marks an unfocused one.

The Simian Line

When a single line slices across the hand in place of the head line and the heart line, that single line is called the Simian line, or Simian crease. ("Simian" means related to monkeys.) The line received its flattering name because someone thought monkeys had this line too. This anonymous namer, however, had never seen an ape up close. Monkeys do not have simian lines. It was once

The Simian
line

thought (probably by the same people who thought all simians had simian lines) that since the simian line looks like a monkey's hand it must be a regressive sign in human hands, and, therefore, must be a stage in every embryo's development. Once again, no luck. The simian line is formed in early prenatal life and stays that way throughout life. So if you have one, learn to like it.

Interpretations of the simian line vary, and none of them are very complimentary. English palmist Fred Gettings claims that simianites are likely to be either criminals or religious fanatics. He says that both of these groups seek extreme solutions to ease their inner tensions. My sense is that the line shows an incapacity to distinguish clearly between the heart and the mind. This leads to tremendous confusion and inner struggle and can make a person cerebral when the moment calls for passion and sentimental when common sense is required. Simianites never quite know what's appropriate.

The simian crease is also a classic symptom of Down's syndrome (mongolism), since it, along with a very small thumb, is prominent sign of that condition. People with Down's syndrome are severely retarded, both mentally and in physical growth. They are very kind, patient people, but intelligence is not their strong point. Not everyone who has a simian crease is tiny or retarded. An important clue is that if someone *cares* whether he has a simian crease, he probably does not have Down's syndrome.

The Fate Line: Not so Fickle

The Fate Line is the vertical line which runs parallel to the life line. Although not everyone has one, it is considered a major line because of the stability its presence imparts to the hand. Although you can live without it, it's better to have it than not, since the fate line represents career, family, or whatever activities give a sense of structure to the life. Without it, one will drift along, and may succeed at many tasks, but will never feel the certainty that he has found his true path. The fate line also indicates attitudes toward success. If it is strong and well-defined the person perseveres until his desires become real. If it is weak or shaky, he lacks commitment, energy, or both. A strong fate line indicates an inner feeling of security which can come from strong family ties, a

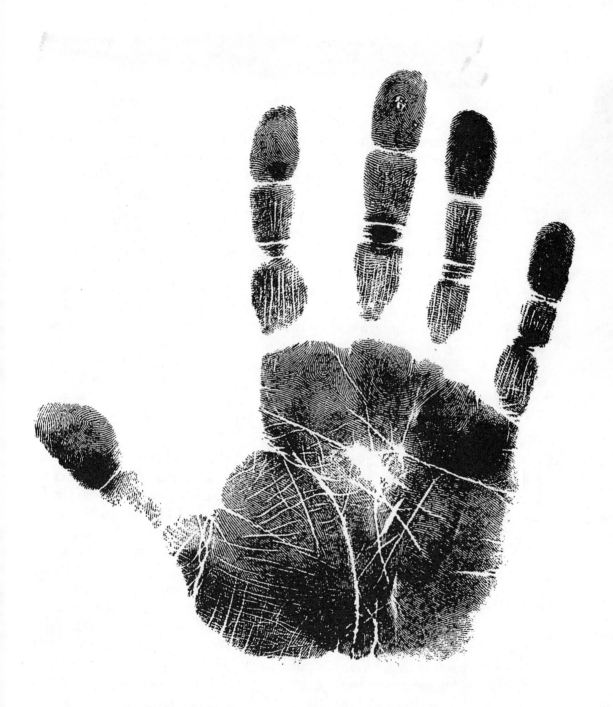

In the hand of television star Robert Walden we see a fate line ending in Jupiter. This shows that he is a natural entertainer.

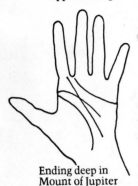

Ending deep in
Mount of Jupiter

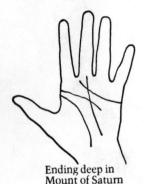

Ending deep in
Mount of Saturn

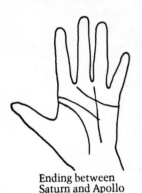

Ending between
Saturn and Apollo

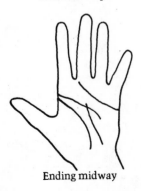

Ending midway

steady job or a feeling that one is "on the right track." Fortunately, even if we lack this innate tendency to feel secure, we can create it.

In many ways, the fate line is like the rudder of a boat. When the rudder moves slightly the boat changes course. Slight shifts in the position of the fate line also indicate a change in the direction of the life. This can be a change in job, or even something more drastic such as a new career or marriage. The position of the boat's rudder is determined by two major factors: the will of the captain and the weather. You are the captain of your life. Your family background and your culture are your port of origin, and your current situation, including the political, social and economic trends of the time, is the weather.

The position and condition of your fate line show how you are adjusting the course of your life. If your intention to succeed is low and the whole world seems to work against you, then your fate line will probably be weak. Conversely, if your will to succeed is strong, the fate line will back you up. This is because the line reflects your attitudes. A skillful captain guides his ship through inclement weather by adapting to the currents as he keeps his destination constantly in mind. So if your life is drifting off course, adjust your rudder.

Like all lines, fate lines can change. Lines on the hands change when you change your life, so focusing your intention on what you want can deepen your fate line as it increases your likelihood for success. (You cannot, however, change your life by changing your lines—don't get a line job to make yourself Super Palm.) People often bemoan their fates as though they had nothing to do with them. Believing that the lines cannot be changed only feeds this delusion. If someone resists the natural direction of his own talents or is unwilling to see the lessons in his daily experience, he might get the impression that success is evading him, when in fact, he is evading success. He might blame his fate, if not his fate line, for dealing him such a lousy hand. But, if he is tone-deaf and trying to be an opera star or is unwilling to train himself in the areas he has natural talent for, then he is dealing his own hand, and if he loses, then he has lost by himself. Look at your fate line. Are you working with it or against it?

The upper end of the fate line, closer to the fingers, represents the career during early life. The end closer to the palm is where you get the engraved gold watch. More important than chronology, however, is the the location of the beginning and ending points of this line. These tell you in what areas of work you are most likely to excel. Here are the variations of the *fate line*:

Lower Endings

Ending mid-palm
between Venus and Luna

Upper Endings:

Location	*Meaning*
Ending deep in the Mount of Jupiter	Career in the public eye. Could be a career in the performing arts or in other fields including teaching, sales, or public speaking. Whatever the details, the underlying motive is the desire to perform.
Ending deep in the Mount of Saturn	Success in whatever one does.
Ending between Saturn and Apollo	Work in a technical aspect of the arts. Could include architecture, drafting or engineering.
Ending midway up the palm	Finds true vocation in midlife (late 20s to 30s, depending on the exact location of the line).

Ending in life line

Lower Endings:

Location	*Meaning*
Ending in the middle of the palm between Venus and Luna	Excellent balance between working for oneself and receiving help from others.
Ending in the life line	Independent business. Success through one's own efforts.
Ending on the Mount of Luna	Helping professions. Willing to receive assistance from others and to give it. Calls on intuition as a practical aid in business.
Extending deep into the Mount of Luna	Deep contact with psychic and spiritual life.

Ending on Mount of
Luna

Ending deep
into Luna

Breaks in the fate line mark the end of a job or a period in the career. If the next segment does not line up with the first segment, the person will change fields when he begins a new job. That is, if the gap is wider, he might move from engineering to movie production rather than from electrical engineering to computer engineering. The closer together the two segments are, the more closely related the two jobs will be. In summary, the fate line is a chart of the movement in a person's career. We speak colloquially of "making a move." When we make a move, our fate line makes a move, too.

Before we proceed to the secondary lines, let us review the Big Four. Everyone has a life line, which records major events and reveals physical stamina. Nearly everyone has both a head line and a heart line. The head line signals mental attitudes and strengths and the heart line reveals emotional history and attitudes toward love. Most people have fate lines, and those who don't lead rudderless lives. Easy. The major lines are like the main streets of the hands—without them we'd be lost. In addition to main thoroughfares, however, side streets are helpful.

The Minor Lines: They Try Harder

Cities are divided into districts—there are shopping districts, residential districts, manufacturing districts, all kinds of districts through which run all kinds of streets. The hands also have good urban planning. Particular areas of the hand contain specific types of energy, and the lines that pass through these areas pick up the related energy and carry it to other parts of the hands. Secondary lines support the main lines by delivering energy to more parts of the hands. The secondary lines fall into two categories, the nameless and the named. When many people have the same minor lines, those lines get names; sometimes they are even named after gods. When a line appears only on the hands of one person, it is unique, and thus it has no special name. If you want to, you can name your secondary lines yourself. How about "Fido"? A multitude of lines scattered all over the hand shows a highstrung temperament. Other secondary lines have more precise meanings.

The named minor lines are: the Line of Apollo, the Health Line, the Inter Life Line, the Marriage Line(s), and the line(s) of

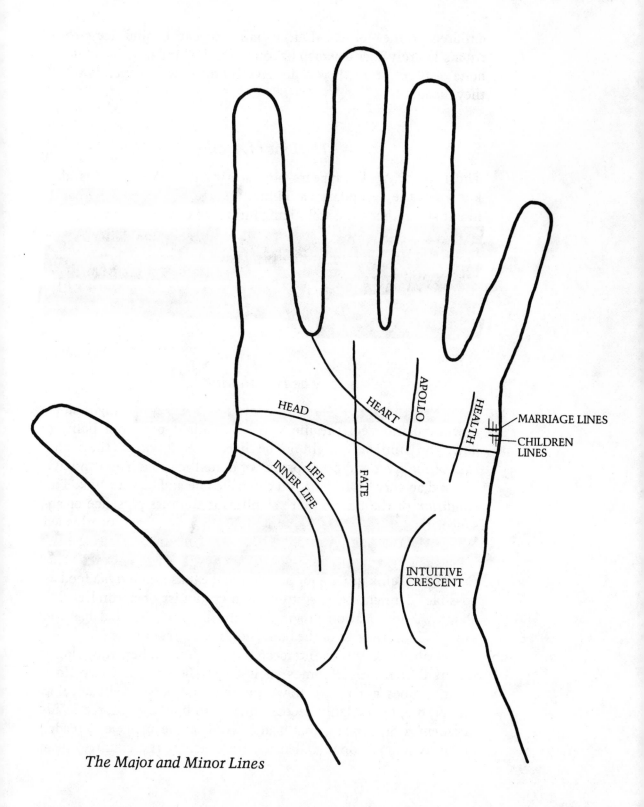

HEAD

HEART

APOLLO

HEALTH

MARRIAGE LINES

CHILDREN LINES

LIFE

INNER LIFE

FATE

INTUITIVE CRESCENT

The Major and Minor Lines

children. (Lines of children usually appear behind ice-cream trucks.) Rarely does a person have all of them, and it is fine to have none of them at all. If you do have them, however, here's what they mean:

The Line of Apollo

The Line of Apollo appears on the Mount of Apollo; it is also known as the Secondary Fate Line. When it ends above the heart line it strengthens the stabilizing influence of the fate line and indicates an appreciation for the arts. If the fate line is weak, the Apollo line still makes it stronger. When the line of Apollo dips below the heart line, the person is a professional artist. If the person wants to appreciate art, it's fine to have Apollo end above the heartline, but if he wants to be a professional artist, it should descend below the heart line.

The Health Line

The Health Line begins on the Mount of Mercury. It might slope down and intersect the life line, or it might peter out halfway down the palm, or it might not be there at all. It reflects the condition of the liver and other organs of detoxification. You can have one and be very healthy or you can have one and be very sick. The *condition* of the line is more significant than its presence or absence. If the line is reddish and inflamed, you have overloaded your body with poisons (these could include alcohol, drugs, refined sugar, meat, or environmental toxins) and it's time to clear them out. Drink quite a lot of water and eat as much fresh food as possible. It might be wise to see a nutritionist or natural doctor about a detoxification program. If the line is faint and has the same color as the rest of the hand, don't worry about it.

Health lines often intersect the life line. When they do, it means that health becomes an issue at the time the two lines meet. It does not mean, however, that the person will develop cancer, die, or suddenly become unable to hold a chiropractic adjustment. It just means that health will become an issue. A reader of my first book once called me from across the country, near tears, because a book she had read convinced her that we would die as soon as the health line crossed the life line. Not true, and she lived to tell the tale.

When determining the ultimate effect of the health line on the person's life, look at the life line below the point where the two lines meet. If the life line continues with undiminished strength, the person will recover fully. Unfortunately, if the life line is significantly weaker after the health line hits, then the person's energy will be cut and he will be chronically affected by his illness. When one reads the health line before sickness strikes, one is forewarned, and forewarned is forearmed. It could be that a sickness is inevitable because of genetic predisposition or because that sickness is the only way for you to learn a particular lesson, but people often suffer unnecessarily. If you respond to early cues from your body and adjust your mind and lifestyle in advance, you can prevent many illnesses. Even if you cannot prevent a problem you might recover faster if you listen and respond to the requests of your body.

The Inner Life Line

The Inner Life Line, also known as the Line of Mars, is parallel to the life line on the Mount of Venus. It supports the life line, giving the individual more stamina. Sometimes this support comes from a spiritual teacher or community, and other times it is like a "reserve generator" within the person himself. It rarely runs the full length of the life line, but rather begins at the point where the person most needs help and ends when the life line and other lines are steady and whole. You can live without it, but it's a fortunate line to have. Particularly if the life line is weak or broken, the inner life line can be a godsend.

Anonymous Lines

You can interpret the nameless, unique secondary lines by noting their endpoints. If a line runs from the Mount of Apollo to the fate line, it's an artistic influence in the person's work. If it runs from the Mount of Luna to the Mount of Mercury, the person might write or speak publicly about intuitive insight. If it connects the head line and the heart line, there's a close relationship between sentiment and rationality. The possibilities are infinite, and you can interpret all of them by remembering the districts and main streets of the hands.

Wedding Bells and Baby Shoes

Marriage Lines appear on the side of the hand below the Mercury finger. They are in chronological order, the top line representing the first marriage, the one beneath it marking the second, and so

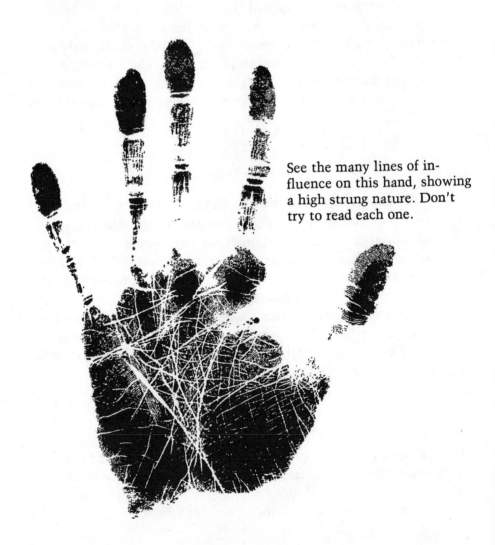

See the many lines of influence on this hand, showing a high strung nature. Don't try to read each one.

forth. They do not always represent marriages, rather they show powerful bonds which might arise between the individual and a mate. The length, depth, color and energy level of each marriage line gives you precise information about the sort of marriage it is, the person's commitment to making the marriage last, and the person's current feelings about the spouse. Remember, however, that the lines show potentiality, not certainty. I once met a Trappist monk who had two marriage lines, and I know a man who was married to the same woman for over sixty years and has several marriage lines. So those of you who have two marriage lines but really like your spouse, take heart. You don't have to trade him or her in.

The length and depth of the marriage lines tell you the basic structure of the marriage. A marriage is like a house: it can be a sturdy brownstone or a tepee. One's feelings about the marriage at a given moment are like the furniture in the house—sometimes it looks great and sometimes it needs redecoration. If the house is well-constructed, it doesn't matter if the drapes clash with the couch for a while. You can redecorate without demoliton. On the other hand, if the roof leaks and the foundations were laid in an oil slick, no decoration will make it feel like home.

A long, deep line is like a snug brick house—it's built to last. It shows that, like it or not, this person will be tied to his mate most of his life. Some people are fortunate to find one person with whom they can share their lives in pleasure and relative peace. Others have several partners, sometimes because they outgrow their early loves and sometimes because they mistakenly believe that a change of partner will eliminate their dissatisfaction with themselves. Some people's partners are claimed by death. Yet, even among people who have several spouses or long relationships, there is usually one relationship which stands out from the others in depth and importance. This relationship is shown by the strongest marriage line.

Shorter marriage lines show shorter relationships and fainter lines show lack of commitment. If the line is long and has no major breaks in it but it looks faint, then the person has a sound marriage that has the blahs. He or she is not putting in the time and commitment to make it work, and the spouse in question might

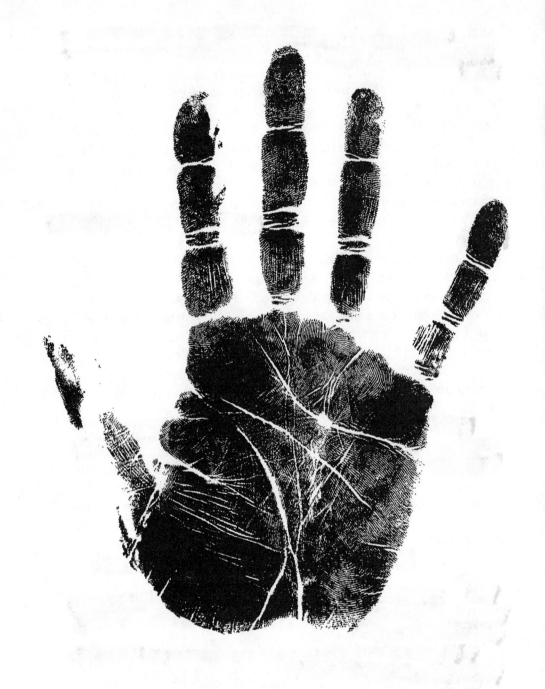

Notice the strong, clear lines in the hand of Damien Simpson, minister and host of *Quest For*, a television show devoted to metaphysics and personal growth.

be losing interest too. If you are in a close relationship and notice your marriage line growing fainter, it means that your commitment is diminishing. If this is what you want, keep it up. If it arises from hurt or unexpressed feelings, then take a chance and share them with your mate. You might see that line grow deep again.

Breaks in the marriage line indicate separations; if the line resumes, so does the marriage.

The color and energy level of the lines give you insight as well. All lines have a color tone which is similar to the natural skin color of the individual. Lines are only considered to have "color" when their color is noticeably different from the rest of the hand. Here are the most common variations in color on the marriage lines.

Redness in or around the lines is a sign of passion and often implies active anger. However, make sure your friend doesn't just have dishpan hands. The redness should appear on some specific part of the line in order to rate as a bona fide message. If the line is red, at least he is fighting out the problems instead of suffering silently.

Darkness on the line is difficult to describe, and is something you will develop a feel for as you read more hands. It usually indicates depression, sullenness, resentment, and so forth, but it can also imply inactivity or an inability to be involved in a relationship at that moment due to forces beyond the individual's control.

White puffy areas around the line indicate uncried tears. Puffy areas on any line on the palm indicate that the person has not yet processed the pain associated with that area in life. If the puffiness extends the length of a marriage line, then the marriage is such a source of misery that he can no longer remember why the marriage took place at all. If there is a brief puffy period, then there is now, or has been in the recent past, a period of heartache from which the person has not yet recovered. Whenever you see this sign, gently remind the person that the only way to get rid of psychological pain is to bring it out into the open and experience it, and that holding it in will only make him sick. Also, if the pain is caused by a relationship, he is being unfair to the partner by never speaking up. Suggest that the person clarify the problem through reflection or talking to a close friend, and then talk it over with

In the hands of Eugene Callender, president of the New York Urban Coalition, adjunct professor of business at Columbia University, and senior minister of the Presbyterian Church of the Master in New York, we see a multitude of lines held in balance by a strong life line. This reflects his ability to excel in many areas of life.

the partner to see if they can come to a better understanding. If a better understanding is impossible or if, for example, the spouse is already dead or has abandoned the person, remind him or her that grief too must be acknowledged and expressed before one can move on to happier possibilities. If there are other people listening, simply tell the person that you could be more specific if you met in private. Then be available to meet in private.

You needn't seek any of these variations in color. If they are there you will notice them immediately. All you need do is open up to your own inner knowledge and let everything else take care of itself. It will.

Reading marriage lines is one area of palmreading in which it pays to be vague. Marriage and longevity are two major areas of self-fulfilling prophecy in people's minds, so emphasize the person's ability to create what happens and down-play the notion of fatalism. In this way you do more service and stay out of a lot more trouble.

Little Lines for Little Ones

The small vertical lines popping up from each marriage line signify children which might be born. The meaning is for "potential children" because many people have dozens of little lines sprouting around their marriage lines, and half of them don't have any children at all, certainly not the twenty or thirty that all those lines would suggest. The only child lines that represent real live babies are the ones that touch the marriage line and are fairly strong and deep. If a person has two marriage lines and the only clear child line comes, for example, from the second line, then he only bears children through his second marriage. Children are born during the marriage on whose line they first appear.

Occasionally a weak child line touches a marriage line which actually does represent a baby, but in this case, the child will be less hearty and strong-willed than the child represented by a clear line springing from a stable marriage. Child lines that almost touch the marriage line represent children who might have been born but didn't quite make it. These include miscarriages, abortions and other forms of incompleted pregnancy. Well-loved stepchildren can also appear as child lines on the hands of the stepparent.

These, then are the lines of the hands: major, minor and anonymous. Some hands have more etchings than a computer chip and others are as clear as tic-tac-toe. Whatever lines you see, you can now understand them, since you are familiar with the major and minor lines as well as the districts of the hands. Thus, you can interpret any line you are handed. Just don't fall for the one about the Brooklyn Bridge.

Review the lines briefly, remembering that each line is a channel of energy. Whenever you read the lines, be sure to see them as parts of the entire hand, including the quadrants, hand shape and posture. When you see everything in context, your interpretation will fall right into line.

5

MANUAL MARKS
AND MOUNTS

In addition to the lines, your hands contain mounts and meaning-ful landmarks. Ancient Rome was laid out around seven major hills and a variety of landmarks. Romans got their bearings accord-ing to how far they were from the Capitoline Hill or the Coliseum. And if it's good enough for the Romans, it's good enough for us. There are eight major mounts on the hands, each one storing a par-ticular type of energy. In addition, there are a series of marks which can appear on any line and a select group of special marks which appear only on the hands of the gifted. As with every other aspect of the hands, mounts and marks can change. Mounts can swell or dwindle, and marks can grow strong or fade. It all depends on you.

Hand Topology, or What's In A Mount

A mount is an area of the palm which is bordered by lines or fingers. That is, if what you are looking at is not a line or a mark or a finger or the very hollow of the hand, it's a mount. Provided you are looking at a hand. Mounts are reservoirs of energy. When they are plump and firm, the person has plenty of the energy associated with that area of the hand; when they are desiccated, that energy is scarce. The firmness of the mounts is almost as important as their plumpness, since the firmness tells you how concentrated or focused the energy is. People with plump, flabby mounts might have plenty of potential energy, but they are letting it all hang out, usually in the form of vague speech, imprecise thought and physical inactivity. These people often overeat sweets and carbohydrates, which intensifies their sense of being weighted with mental and physical sludge. Thus, a firm, moderately high mount is preferable to a flabby, high one.

Before examining the mounts any further, here are a few words about judging mount size. When reading palms it pays to be observant, but not rigid. There are no strict standards of measure. There is just your observation, your intelligence and your intuition. And that is enough. If you are looking for a Mountometer to say, "Bingo! Big Mount!" when you press it against your hand, you won't find it. Fortunately, you don't need it. Look at the whole hand, even the whole body, and get a sense of its proportion. Look at the hand and see which mounts strike you as being bigger or smaller than the others, given the whole body proportion and the look of the hand. You already know what is big and what is small. Don't lose contact with your instinctive knowledge just because you are learning a new subject.

For those of you whose concern is still mounting, however, I shall share a bit of deep esoteric knowledge with you. The more mounts stick up from the hand, the bigger they are.

One exciting aspect of studying the mounts is that they can change very rapidly. The height and firmness of the mounts tells you how well stocked you are with particular types of energy. Look at your hands now. Notice all their hills and valleys, and get a sense of the height and firmness of the mounts. How are you feeling? Happy? Sad? Tired? God forbid, bored? Remember how your hands look to you now. Then look at them again later today or in a few days, particularly at a moment when you are bursting with energy or exhausted. You will see a striking difference. If you always feel the same, then try to gun up some energy or wear yourself out, just to see the difference. (Anything for science . . .)

Meanings of the Mounts

There are eight major mounts on each hand. All are named after Greek or Roman gods or goddesses, just like the fingers. In fact,

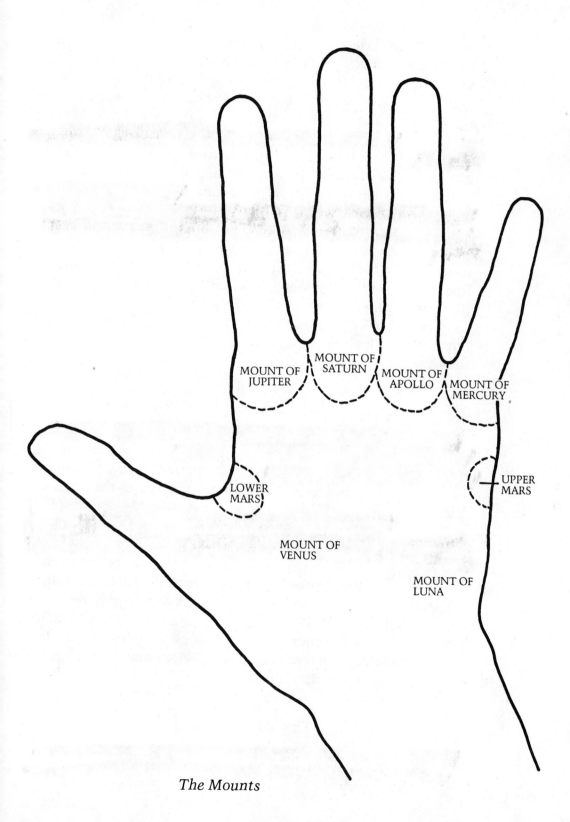

MOUNT OF
JUPITER

MOUNT OF
SATURN

MOUNT OF
APOLLO

MOUNT OF
MERCURY

LOWER
MARS

UPPER
MARS

MOUNT OF
VENUS

MOUNT OF
LUNA

The Mounts

four of them have the same patron deities as the fingers, which means that you've already learned half of the mounts. Wasn't that easy? The mounts under Saturn and Apollo have little significance as individual mounts since the area they take up is the location of the Girdle of Venus. (This girdle represents added sensitivity and affection.) A high Mount of Jupiter indicates prosperity on a practical hand. When combined with powerful influences from Luna and other special marks (such as the Ring of Solomon), it can also indicate a capacity for spiritual leadership. A flat Mount of Jupiter implies trouble in paying the bills. An inflated Mount of Mercury shows writing talent; if it is too puffed up, this talent is not being used. (When the mount overflows with energy, it shows that the energy is not being permitted to leave its reservoir and circulate freely.) An overflowing Mercury mount topped by a skinny little Mercury finger is a sure sign of writer's block.

The other major mounts are Venus, Luna, Upper Mars and Lower Mars. Of all the mounts on the hands, Venus and Luna are the most significant.

The Mount of Venus

The Mount of Venus is the same as the passive/receptive/outer quadrant, but it sounds much more romantic. It is the reservoir of physical vitality and sensuality. In Greek mythology, Venus was the desired and desiring goddess of love. She is also the queen of laughter. A Mount of Venus which is high and firm in proportion to the rest of the hand shows good resistance to sickness, a hearty and enthusiastic appreciation of physical things, and an affectionate nature. A dry or stringy looking Mount of Venus shows that the person is either repressing his natural exuberance or is suffering from a chronic illness. Both conditions can be improved by a healthy dose of love. Particularly if you are starting a new romance, you can see your Mount of Venus blossom from Venus Gulch into Mount Everest's twin sister. When your juices begin to boil, Venus always perks up.

The Mount of Luna

The Mount of Luna comprises the passive/receptive/inner quadrant, and thus represents the source of our inner-directed energy.

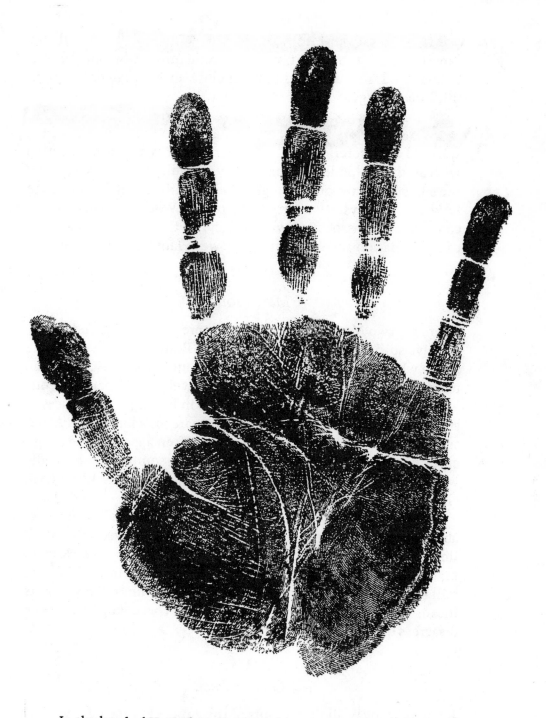

In the hand of Yogi Bhajan, spiritual leader of Sikh Dharma in the Western World, we see a powerful dynamism, a Mystic Triangle, and deep grounding in Venus and Luna.

It is the home of our intuitive or subconscious mind. Since all our experience is both conditioned and remembered by our subconscious mind, it is essential to be in close and loving contact with this lunar energy.

Luna is the goddess of the moon. She affects the tides, and so is associated with long voyages. Luna is also the patroness of the spiritual and esoteric arts. This is part of her symbolic connection with all that is hidden during the day. (Traditionally, daylight and the sun suggest rational thought, and nighttime and the moon are linked to the mysterious irrational mind.) When Luna gets out of control, she is associated with lunacy, or the inability to control the imagination and differentiate between fantasy and reality.

Mars Mounts

There are two Mounts of Mars. Both represent courage and the aggressive spirit associated with Mars, the Roman god of war. Upper Mars, which is found just under the Mount of Mercury, is like an underground reservoir of stubborn perseverance. When someone with a strong Mount of Upper Mars digs in her heels and refuses to surrender, her opponents had better prepare for a long siege. A person with a strong Mount of Upper Mars often appears to be adaptable and easygoing, but just oppose her in something she really wants to do and you'll see her clinging to her goals like lichen clings to a rock. Think donkey.

A person with a strong Mount of Lower Mars is less discreet about her stubbornness. Lower Mars is found between the headline and the thumb, tucked into the Mount of Venus. In Roman mythology, Venus and Mars were enraptured lovers and they are still side by side here on the hand. A strong Mount of Lower Mars means that this person will actively resist those with whom she disagrees or who obstruct her will.

On the Quad

If you take away all the mounts of the hand, the area left over will be the *Quadrangle*, or the Plain of Mars. This is colloquially known as the "hollow of the palm" and is associated with candy which does not melt. At least not there. There is an old Chinese story about a master of Tai Ch'i Chuan (an ancient system of meditation in motion) who once trapped a small bird in the hollow of his hand. His sensitivity and subtlety of movement were so refined that every time the bird tried to take off by pressing against his hand, he lowered his quadrangle just enough to equal the weight of the bird. Unable to find any resistance, the bird had to stay in the palm of the master's hand.

Apart from its use as a launching pad, the hollow of the palm reflects the temperament. A deeply hollowed quadrangle shows an extremely sensitive nature.

The Marks Brothers

In addition to the lines and mounts, you might also find marks on the hands. These can appear in or around the lines. Learn to read the marks and you can read between the lines. When marks appear on the lines, they represent obstructions or modifications of the energy which is carried in the line or mount on which they appear. That is, marks in the life line show changes in the life; marks on the head line show changes in the mind, and so forth. There are eight different marks which can appear anywhere in the hand:

Note the health line, Mystic Cross, and square enclosing the head line in the hand of Michael Hughes, an eminent psychic.

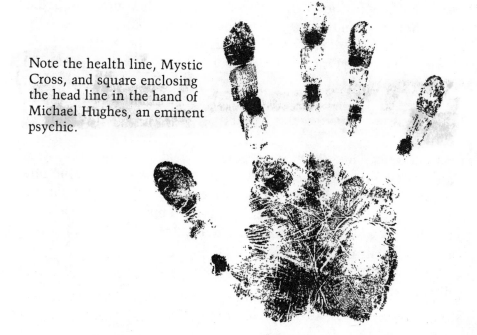

Chains, Islands, Bars, Crosses, Triangles, Squares and Grids. Each has a general meaning of its own plus a specific meaning depending on where in the hand it appears. In addition, there are four special marks which always appear in the same place on the hands and whose meaning is constant.

Marks on the lines give you detailed information about events in the person's life, but they do not outweigh the influence of the basic temperament and trend of life as shown by the hand shape and the path of the major lines. That is, marks on the lines might represent events or periods of life—things that happen to us—but the things that happen to us do not alter our original nature. Special marks, however, do show qualities which are inherent in our character. These are the marks that appear on the lines:

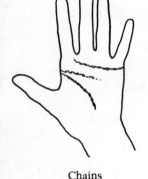

Chains

The Chained Gang

Suppose you are barreling down Route 66, all six lanes wide open and your car in fifth gear, when suddenly you hit a stretch where there are beer cans and flat tires all over the road. This might slow you down. Similarly, if the lines of a hand are chained or broken up, energy cannot flow freely along them. This gives the person a feeling of confusion or disruption in his life. If you see a chained life line on a hand where other lines are in good shape, then this person's clear head and healthy heart are keeping his nerves under control; however, it's probably an uphill battle. If the heart line is chained, the person is insecure and easily hurt in love. If the head line is chained, it is hard for the person to remain focused on any subject; he is forever wandering into depressing or confused trains of thought.

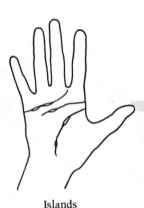

Islands

Tasseled lines indicate a gradual weakening of the powers associated with the line. This is most often found in the life line, where a tasseling at the end indicates that the person's vitality wanes gradually as he approaches old age. This is no surprise. It's a rare person who has the good luck to run straight into death after a long and healthy life.

Wavy lines mean that the person is incapable of taking a direct route to anywhere.

No Man Is an Island, But on the Other Hand . . .

Like wide center dividers on a super highway, islands divide the flow of energy on the line in half and thus weaken the force of each side. Islands on the life line indicate a period of divided energy or ambivalence. They can also represent a period when the person wanted to do one thing but was forced by circumstances to do another.

Up To The Bar

Suppose a huge truck overturns on the freeway and spills lead pipes across all the lanes. Now imagine trying to drive your motorcycle through without slowing down—could be trouble. Bars are like complete obstructions across the freeway of your life. Fortunately, you can be your own Highway Patrol and clean up the mess yourself. Bars restrict the flow of energy more than any other mark, but there are several good things about them. First, they represent brief, specific problems rather than chronic conditions. Therefore, even though they are not fun, at least they are fast. Second, we learn a lot by passing through them, or leaping over them, or making them disappear, or whatever we do to get past them. Bars can signify major illnesses, ends of close relationships, or getting fired from a job, depending on which major line they visit. As long as the line continues beyond the bar, you'll recover from whatever distress or upset the bar represents.

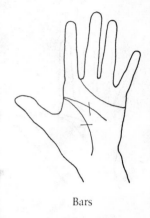

Bars

In rare cases, the line will be weakened for the rest of its length after being crossed by a bar. This is more serious, as it means that the difficulty has a permanent dampening effect on one's vitality. Be extremely watchful as that period of life approaches, and remember that you create your reality through your fears and beliefs. Experience your fears, acknowledge your beliefs, and decide that whatever happens will be in your best interest. At the very least, this will keep you distracted while disaster strikes.

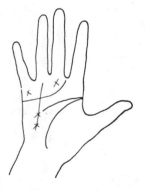

Crosses

Cross Your Hands

Crosses on the lines generally have the same meaning as crosses on an answer to a test. Wrong. They show that fate seems to be working against you at the time the cross appears. Once again, these are temporary disturbances which usually have long-term benefits. Some palmreaders claim that a cross on the Mount of Saturn is a good sign, but I cannot confirm this. A couple of crosses will neither save nor destroy a person's life, so don't be cross if you have one.

Triangles

Although social triangles create confusion, palmistic triangles create peace. Triangles have a calming influence on the energy of the mount or line on which they appear. For example, on the Mount of Venus, triangles imply restraint of passion. On Jupiter, the calming influence of the triangle enables the person to have greater influence on the people around him. A triangle over any of the major lines shows special spiritual protection during the period of the person's life represented by that section of that line. All in all, triangles are great.

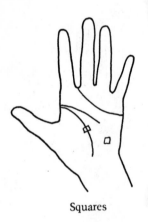

Triangles

Be Square

Squares do not always fall within a line; they are more likely to be spread over a particular line or area of the hand. They are marks of protection and preservation from harm. If there is a break in any of the lines and the break is covered by a square, then the person will be protected from feeling the full negative effects of whatever mischance, whether it be illness, accident, or freak-out, that the break in the line represents. Some people say that squares are signs of preservation springing from a spiritual force; others say the protection comes from the person's own inner resources. Your interpretation should depend on the message you receive from the individual hand.

Squares

There is one startling thing about hands on which squares appear. The squares last only as long as they are needed. I have seen many hands in which one of the lines had a break in it or became extremely weak and in which a square extended throughout the period where the main line was weak, broken or tasseled. At the point in the line (and therefore in the life) when the pain that caused the break was healed, the square just melted away.

Hominy Grids

Grids amplify the skills or tendencies associated with the mounts on which they are found. If you have grids, beware lest you get too much of a good thing. Energy on mounts that have grids is not channeled as it is on the lines, so it may be hard to regulate. Particularly if the grids appear on the Mount of Venus, enjoy yourself—carefully. When they appear on the Mount of Apollo, grids show a diffusion of artistic interest which may lead to dilettantism. People with gridded Apollo mounts might even be so scattered that they are dilettante dilettantes.

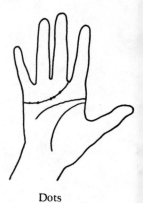

Dots

Dot Dot Dot

Dots are temporary blockages of energy. They may signify a depression if found on the head or heart line, or they might indicate minor illnesses if found on the life line. On the fate line, they reflect temporary problems at the office. Your intuitive self will inform you about the exact reasons for these minor hindrances.

If a series of dots appears on the head line it shows a chronic cycle of depression: Feeling good, then back in the pits, feeling good, then back in the pits, an endless treadmill of disturbance. This might be caused by low blood sugar, but it is best dealt with by a professional counselor.

A series of dots on the heart line shows a series of disastrous love affairs. Encourage the individual to look for the pattern that ties her miseries together. Did they *all* wear polka dot ties? Observing what the relationships and partners have in common will make it easier to avoid making the same mistake again.

One final note about marks. You don't *have* to have them. In fact, no one has all of them, and many happy people are padding around the planet with none of them at all. So, if you see them, read them, and if you don't, don't worry.

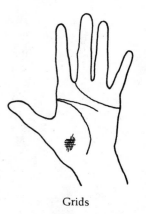

Grids

Special Marks

The special marks are independent of the lines and mounts. They include the Girdle of Venus, the Intuitive Crescent (a breakfast roll that reads the future?), the Mystic Triangle and the Ring of

Solomon. Less significant special marks are the Marks of Inheritance and the Healer's Marks. Most of these marks appear in the upper, or active, half of the hand. To make learning them simpler, we'll trace them from quadrant to quadrant, beginning with the active/outer quadrant and moving clockwise around the hand.

The Ring of Solomon

The only special mark in this quadrant is the Ring of Solomon, which is a semicircle on the Mount of Jupiter. When fully developed, it forms a complete ring around the base of the Jupiter finger. It symbolizes spiritual leadership—the ability to guide others charismatically on the path to higher knowledge. Legend has it that no one was permitted to work on Solomon's temple unless he had this mark on his hands.

Partially formed rings are more common than fully formed ones, just as partially enlightened teachers are more common than true masters. These partial rings show that a person is progressing toward the level at which she will be able to teach, but has not yet arrived.

Venus and the Triangle

Two important marks bridge the area between the active/outer and the active/inner quadrants: The Girdle of Venus and the Mystic Triangle. The Girdle of Venus enhances the sensitivity and emotional awareness of its bearer. This heightened awareness usually leads to greater compassion in all the person's activities. When the girdle is deep and makes a complete semicircle between the Mounts of Saturn and Mercury, the person is too sensitive for her own good. She takes things too much to heart and is emotionally restless. Wounded deeply by the pinpricks of others, she roams constantly looking for something that will ease her restless heart. When the girdle is composed of several interwoven lines, however, sensitivity is strong and growing but is still grounded in pragmatic acceptance of daily life.

The Mystic Triangle is located between the head and heart lines in the center of the palm. It implies skill in the occult or psychic arts. If one side of the triangle is formed by the fate line, then the person's entire life will be influenced by her aptitude for psychic awareness. Many people want to think that they have Mystic Triangles, but we only accept the real thing. Like all triangles, this must have three distinct angles; otherwise it's just a few lines of influence meandering across the quadrangle. True Mystic Triangles are not common.

Sometimes the space which would be taken up by the Mystic Triangle is filled by a distinct cross which is called, not surprisingly, the Mystic Cross. It also represents skill and interest in psychic skills, although it does not have quite the same force as the Mystic Triangle.

Healers and Heirs

The Marks of Inheritance are small vertical lines which appear in the crook between the Apollo and Mercury fingers. They sometimes look like the far end of a Girdle of Venus, but they are not. You can tell the difference because the Apollo end of the girdle tends to curve toward the Mount of Saturn, whereas the Marks of Inheritance are straight. As their name implies, they indicate that the person will inherit money or other valuable goods. The deeper the lines, the surer (and fatter) the inheritance.

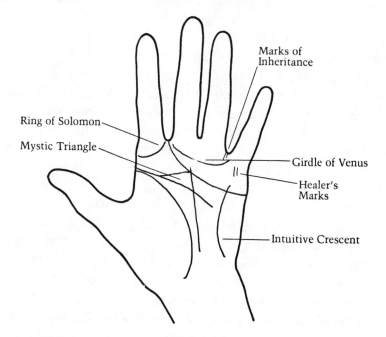

Healer's Marks are a series of small vertical lines on the Mount of Mercury. Although few professional healers have them, they often appear on the hands of people who are in the helping professions, including nurses, teachers, and psychotherapists, and among kindly mothers and fathers. People who have these marks are notable because everyone feels better when they are around. A hug from from someone with Healer's Marks goes further than a hug from someone without them. However, if someone without the marks wants to hug you, don't be picky. Hug her back.

Intuitive Croissant?

The last special mark is the Intuitive Crescent, which appears on the Mount of Luna. It represents gut intuition. A client once told me about her father, a no-nonsense blue collar worker who stoutly denied that any psychic phenomena existed, and who snarled at anyone who intimated that he might have such abilities himself. He wan't *psychic*, he said— he just knew when things were going to happen. He had a deep, clear Intuitive Crescent.

On an earthy or simple hand, this mark shows a tendency to respond from the gut rather than from the mind or heart. While this is an asset in certain situations, such as stalking wild elephants or walking home alone at 3:00 A.M., it can also be a liability. Now and then someone gets a gut instinct to punch someone in the nose. In the short run this might be exciting, but in the long run it's more productive to channel that instinct through the more refined parts of the character such as compassion and the intellect before letting it loose. By doing this the person with the Intuitive Crescent can use the knowledge it gives him without getting in trouble. On gentler (more conic or pointed) hands, the Crescent shows a strong gut intuition tempered by the more forgiving aspects of the character.

If you have the Ring of Solomon, the Girdle of Venus, Marks of Inheritance, Healer's Marks or the Intuitive Crescent, that's wonderful. And if you don't have them, you can still be wise, sensitive, compassionate, rich, helpful and intuitive. You'll just have to focus on those qualities more in order to experience them.

With this exposition of fundamental palmistry, you have learned to understand the quadrants, the hand shapes, the postures and tension patterns of the hands. You have also mastered the variations in the major and the minor lines, as well as in the mounts and marks. Moreover, you have learned to watch the changes in your own hands and the hands of your friends as your mood and energy levels vary. We could finish with palmistry here and be content to know the basics, but let's not. You have learned the basic vocabulary of the hands, and now you can begin to write poems.

Please take a moment to look over the previous chapters and make sure that your grasp of them is firm before you move to the next step: using palmreading to improve your personal relationships.

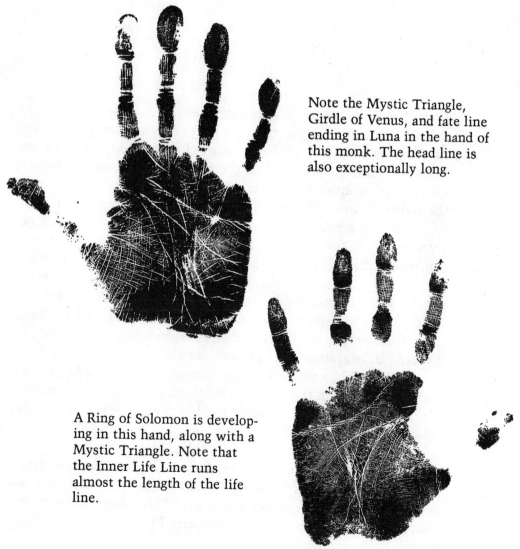

Note the Mystic Triangle, Girdle of Venus, and fate line ending in Luna in the hand of this monk. The head line is also exceptionally long.

A Ring of Solomon is developing in this hand, along with a Mystic Triangle. Note that the Inner Life Line runs almost the length of the life line.

6

COMPATIBILITY
AND THE HANDS

Love. Everyone wants it, everyone needs it, and although universal love is great, it's a lot more fun to get down to specifics. We all meet many people in our lives. Most of them are great folks, but we don't fall in love with all of them. Nor do we work easily with all of them, want to be friends with all of them, nor even let all of them drink from our cups without wiping their mouths. In some cases, seeing a person once is enough to last us the rest of our lives. So, even though there is a universal love which ultimately unifies all differences, differences certainly appear to arise. When we like or can accept the differences between ourselves and others, we are compatible with them. When the differences between us make us foam at the mouth, we are incompatible. Fortunately, the very qualities which one person considers grounds for divorce can be aphrodisiacs to someone else.

Compatibility palmistry uses the interpretation of five compatibility factors in the hands to help you gauge your compatibility with another person. It can be used in choosing and coping with co-workers and in selecting friends. In both of these areas it will help you run your life more smoothly. The area closest to the heart, however, is love. Close, intimate love. How can we attract it and whom should we choose? And how can we maintain freshness without sealing the inner wrapper? These are questions that concern nearly everyone, and compatibility palmistry can help provide the answers.

In this chapter we'll examine five aspects of the hands which give you insight into your compatibility with another person. They are the:

- Hand Shape
- Heart Line
- Thumb
- Mount of Venus
- Marriage Line(s)

The hand shape reflects the temperament, the heart line shows basic emotional attitudes, the thumb shows strength of will, the Mount of Venus shows sexual drive, and the marriage lines show how many (if any) long-term emotional commitments the person is likely to have.

Among these five factors, the first two are essential, that is, compatibility in these areas is a prerequisite for even a fairly satisfying relationship. Harmony in the next two areas is helpful, and compatibility on the last factor is a bonus. If your hand shapes, and hence your fundamental temperaments, are radically out of balance, odds are you will always feel alienated from each other. If your heart lines, and therefore your basic emotional values, are incompatible, you're likely to cause each other pain because of your different expectations about the relationship. The pain caused by the expression of fundamental incompatibilities is often unintentional; it's a product of each person being himself. If your basic characters are incompatible, there's not a whole lot you can do to make the relationship pleasant and long-lasting.

For example, if I'm basically outgoing and you're basically clingy, you'll feel hurt when I talk to everyone at the party (even though I don't mean anything by it), and I'll be astounded when you accuse me of being fickle or inattentive. Certainly, we could compromise (I could promise to check in with you every fifteen minutes, but how boring), yet even with compromise, possessiveness would always be an issue for us. Many great differences can be overcome through communication and love, but fundamental mismatches of values or temperament are hard to conquer.

There will always be cases in which none of your factors is compatible and yet you still fall madly in love. As Pascal said, "The heart has its reasons which reason knows not." If you have to fall in love, you'll fall in love, with or without compatibility palmistry. This chapter is not about translating love into an actuarial table, it's about knowing oneself and one's partner and playing the odds.

You are about to discover a unique tool called the Hand Compatibility Chart, which will help you gauge your basic compatibility with another person. Although you alone will make the final choice of who receives your favors, the chart will give you a sense of what the strong points in the relationship will be, along with the areas in which you're most likely to disagree. Of course you can go ahead and marry someone with whom you're incompatible—a lot of people do—but at least you'll have an inkling of what you're in for.

The principles in the Compatibility Chart can also be applied to your relationships with friends, family and co-workers. Although all five factors are important, the significance of each factor varies according to which type of relationship you'd like to have. For example, differences in sex drive are less likely to create problems between parents and small children than between the two parents.

What Is Compatibility?

Is it more than just holding hands? Before you can be compatible with someone else, you must be compatible with yourself. This includes having an awareness of which habits in other people make you rabid and which ones make you glad. It also includes knowing what your strong points are and in what areas you need support from your loved ones, as well as knowing what kind of support you're able to give. Being compatible with yourself also means knowing that you don't need a constant companion to be a complete person. It might be fun, but you don't need it. All of us have learned from dismal experience that when we look for a companion because we're starved for love, we don't get one. And the instant we stop looking for it, that charming mate walks in the front door. Right here, right now, with nothing added, each one of us is enough.

Although cosmic self-sufficiency is great, it does not fill up the other half of the bed. Nor does it take out the trash, go to the movies with you, or bring you soup when you're sick. Being complete within yourself does not mean that you should do everything by or for yourself. If you were meant to do everything for yourself, there wouldn't be all these other people on the planet. So enjoy! In the process of loving other people we can discover our inner potential for love. What's important is to recognize that our happiness does not depend on any other person or circumstance: We create it ourselves. Knowing that, we can truly enjoy the company of those we love without blame, anxiety, or fear that they only love us for our chicken salad sandwich.

Compatibility is based on complementary characteristics and awareness of oneself and one's partner. Balance each other's excesses wherever possible, and be conscious about your potential areas of friction. Do this, and you might be able to start your own "Love Boat." One basic principle is the foundation of all the compatibility guidelines in this book: *Look for someone different enough from you so that you complement each other, yet similar enough so that you feel comfortable. Be different, but not too different.*

The five compatibility factors in your hands give you information about the person which might not be apparent at first blush (or even at first kiss), so you can use them to spare yourself a lot of trouble. Armed with these five factors, you might pluck Cupid's arrow from an unwary breast or give a near-miss a second chance. By comparing the meaning of these factors on your own hands to the same factors on the hands of your friend, you can picture the form your relationship is likely to have.

The Hand in Hand Compatibility Checklist will make this process much easier for you. The scores are weighted differently for couples, co-workers and friends because the same characteristics that make you fond friends might make you discontented lovers. The guidelines give you a sense of the strongest areas of your relationships, as well as highlighting the areas that will require the most compromise. The checklist is a tool for understanding each other better, not a scorecard. So have fun with it, and may the best man win.

You might enjoy reading it with a friend or lover, so that you can practice compatibility while I preach it.

The Compatibility Factors

Each of the compatibility factors is also a regular part of the hand. That is, you don't suddenly sprout an extra finger when you meet the one you love. These factors become compatibility factors because they represent aspects of our character which strongly affect the way we relate to other people. Reviewing them briefly in the context of compatibility, the five factors are hand shape, heart line ending, thumb flexibility, Mount of Venus and marriage line(s). The hand shape and the ending of the heart line must be compatible, or you will have to grapple with fundamental conflicts in values and temperament. It's helpful if the thumb and the Mount of Venus are in similar proportion, since that means you'll be evenly matched both in arguments and in bed. (Even if you argue in bed you'll be well matched.) If you both have the same number of marriage lines *and* the same number of previous marriages, it will be easier to agree on how much commitment you both desire. We'll begin with the two essential factors: hand shape and ending of the heart line.

Hand Shape

The hand shape reflects the basic temperament. Recall that a square hand shows practicality, a conic hand shows adaptibility, a pointed hand shows idealism and sensitivity, and a spatulate hand shows dynamism. If your hands are too different, the two of you will be like air and earth, one heading up and the other heading down. If they're too similar, you'll feel like you married your twin. The difficulty with having incompatible hand shapes is that there's very little you can do to remedy the problem. Adaptations can be made in sex drive, rigidity of will, and ability to commit oneself, but certain characteristics, such as natural speed of movement and thought, practicality, and stamina are not likely to be completely transformed. If you are temperamentally mismatched, your road to happiness will run right up the front of a rocky cliff, with few toeholds to aid you. On the positive side, if you are well matched in temperament, you can pass through many conflicts with your communication and love intact.

When choosing the person to whom you will give your hand, look for someone whose hand shape is neither too similar nor too

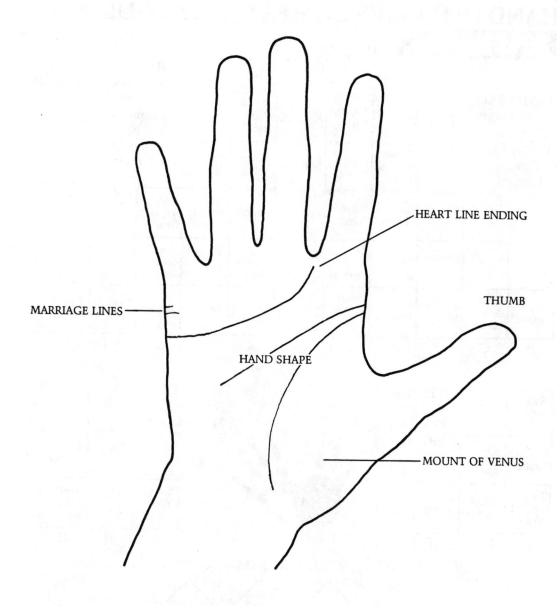

HEART LINE ENDING

MARRIAGE LINES

THUMB

HAND SHAPE

MOUNT OF VENUS

Compatibility Factors

Hand Shape—Temperament
Heart Line Ending—Emotional Attitudes
Thumb—Strength of Will
Mount of Venus—Sexuality and Stamina
Marriage Lines—Number of Commitments

HAND IN HAND'S COMPATIBILITY GUIDE FOR
FRIENDS

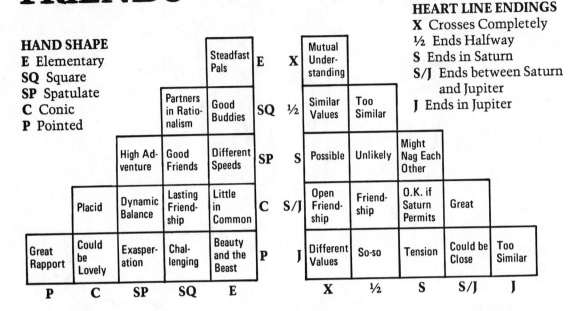

HAND SHAPE
- **E** Elementary
- **SQ** Square
- **SP** Spatulate
- **C** Conic
- **P** Pointed

	P	C	SP	SQ	E
E					Steadfast Pals
SQ				Partners in Rationalism	Good Buddies
SP			High Adventure	Good Friends	Different Speeds
C		Placid	Dynamic Balance	Lasting Friendship	Little in Common
P	Great Rapport	Could be Lovely	Exasperation	Challenging	Beauty and the Beast

HEART LINE ENDINGS
- **X** Crosses Completely
- **½** Ends Halfway
- **S** Ends in Saturn
- **S/J** Ends between Saturn and Jupiter
- **J** Ends in Jupiter

	X	½	S	S/J	J
X	Mutual Understanding				
½	Similar Values	Too Similar			
S	Possible	Unlikely	Might Nag Each Other		
S/J	Open Friendship	Friendship	O.K. if Saturn Permits	Great	
J	Different Values	So-so	Tension	Could be Close	Too Similar

THUMB
- **R** Rigid
- **FLX** Flexible
- **FPY** Floppy

	R	FLX	FLP
R	Rousing Arguments		
FLX	Happiness Possible	Easy-going Pals	
FLP	Dominant/Submissive	Could Be Fun	Boring

MOUNT OF VENUS
- **H** High
- **M** Moderate
- **F** Flat

	F	M	H
H			White Water Rapids
M		Placid Pals	Great Balance
F	Share Your Geritol	Very Quiet	Energy Imbalance

MARRIAGE LINES

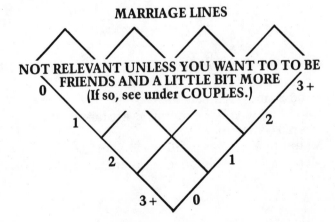

NOT RELEVANT UNLESS YOU WANT TO TO BE FRIENDS AND A LITTLE BIT MORE (If so, see under COUPLES.)

0   3+
1   2
2   1
3+   0

HAND IN HAND'S COMPATIBILITY SCORING FOR
FRIENDS

To calculate your innate compatibility with a friend or a person you would like to have as a friend: Look at your own hand and determine its shape. Write your shape in the appropriate blank in the "Your Type" column. Write the shape of your friend's hand in the "Friend's Type" column. On the large chart, opposite left, locate the square that is common to both types; you will get a clue as to the compatibility of your two hand shapes from the words in the square. That clue has a numerical value in the corresponding square in the small chart to the right. Write this number in the appropriate blank in the "Combined Factor Scores" column. Repeat this process with the other Compatibility Factors, taking special note of the first two factors—hand shape and heart line—as they are considered prerequisites for a good relationship. Add up the individual Combined Factor Scores to determine your Total Compatibility Score and check the key at the bottom of the page. Remember that the Compatibility Guide is simply a tool to help you focus your own intuitive sense of what is best for you.

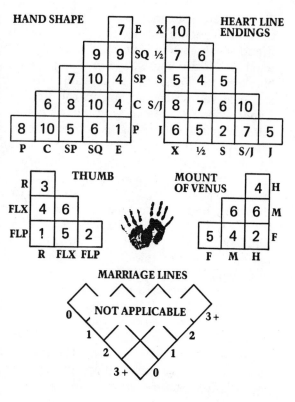

Compatibility Factor	Your Type	Friend's Type	Combined Factor Score
Hand Shape			
Heart Line Ending			
Thumb			
Mount of Venus			
Marriage Lines			
Total Compatibility Score:			

Key to Factor Scores
Hand Shape and Heart Line: 1 No dice. **2** Why bother? **3** Blah. **4** Possible. **5.** Even odds. **6** An improvement. **7** Now you're talking. **8** Good. **9** Very good. **10** Heaven. **Thumb and Mt. of Venus: 1** Trouble. **2** Tepid. **3** You can try... **4** Improving. **5** Very good. **6** Excellent.

Key to Total Score
4–11	Buy a dog instead.
12–19	Better stay acquaintances.
19–26	A growing bond...
27–32	Friends forever.

HAND IN HAND'S COMPATIBILITY SCORING FOR
FRIENDS

To calculate your innate compatibility with a friend or a person you would like to have as a friend: Look at your own hand and determine its shape. Write your shape in the appropriate blank in the "Your Type" column. Write the shape of your friend's hand in the "Friend's Type" column. On the large chart, opposite left, locate the square that is common to both types; you will get a clue as to the compatibility of your two hand shapes from the words in the square. That clue has a numerical value in the corresponding square in the small chart to the right. Write this number in the appropriate blank in the "Combined Factor Scores" column. Repeat this process with the other Compatibility Factors, taking special note of the first two factors—hand shape and heart line—as they are considered prerequisites for a good relationship. Add up the individual Combined Factor Scores to determine your Total Compatibility Score and check the key at the bottom of the page. Remember that the Compatibility Guide is simply a tool to help you focus your own intuitive sense of what is best for you.

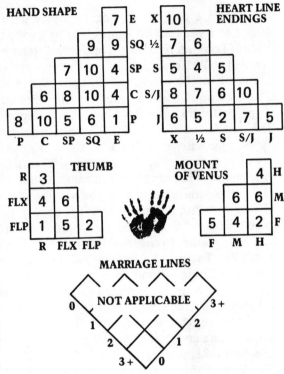

Compatibility Factor	Your Type	Friend's Type	Combined Factor Score
Hand Shape	_____	_____	_____
Heart Line Ending	_____	_____	_____
Thumb	_____	_____	_____
Mount of Venus	_____	_____	_____
Marriage Lines	_____	_____	_____
	Total Compatibility Score:		_____

Key to Factor Scores
Hand Shape and Heart Line: 1 No dice. **2** Why bother? **3** Blah. **4** Possible. **5.** Even odds. **6** An improvement. **7** Now you're talking. **8** Good. **9** Very good. **10** Heaven. **Thumb and Mt. of Venus: 1** Trouble. **2** Tepid. **3** You can try... **4** Improving. **5** Very good. **6** Excellent.

Key to Total Score
4–11	Buy a dog instead.
12–19	Better stay acquaintances.
19–26	A growing bond...
27–32	Friends forever.

different from your own. Two square hands might bore each other to death (how many times can you balance the checkbook?), and two pointed-handed people would be like Hansel and Gretel lost in the forest. Yet a square hand and a pointed hand might find conjugal life exasperating, too, since the pointed-handed partner would always be wounded by the simple directness of the earthbound mate. Look for balance. A square hand would go well with a conic or spatulate hand, and a pointed hand would go well with a conic or slightly spatulate hand. Choose a partner who is strong in your weaker areas and rambunctious where you're too fastidious. Too much similarity leads to boredom and too much difference leads to alienation.

Everyone wants someone with whom he has a lot in common, but who wants to marry his clone? (If you said, "Me," go back to Chapter 1 and keep reading about yourself.) With complementary hand shapes, you and your friends will go far.

Heart Line

The heart line reflects the emotional attitudes and history of the individual. The line's endpoint shows the attitudes and its condition indicates the history. Recall that a chained heart line shows many previous disappointments and difficulty in trusting others' love, and a deep, clear line shows great constancy. The form that the love will take still depends on the line's ending. Some lines end "Happily Ever After" and others are spliced in midplot.

Heart line endings in the Mount of Jupiter show self-centeredness and sometimes possessiveness in love. Endings between Jupiter and Saturn show mature and balanced expectations about close relationships. Endings on the Mount of Saturn show idealism and perfectionism in relationships, and lines ending halfway across the hand show a need for distance—space—in relationships. A heart line that crosses the palm entirely shows humanitarian or nonattached love.

If you and your lover share basic values about commitment and love, then you can feel more secure that he or she will respond to you in ways that make you feel good. If you're a romantic and he's a humanitarian, you might want flowers for your anniversary and he might want to give a donation to the United Way. Sure,

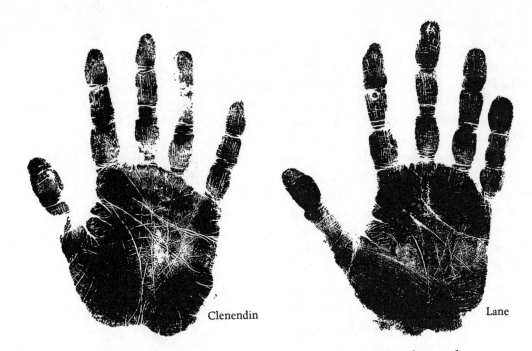

Clenendin

Lane

Golda Clenendin and Shoshana Lane are close friends who work together in Lifechanges, teaching people to use color and clothing as tools for success. Note the compatibility of their hand shapes.

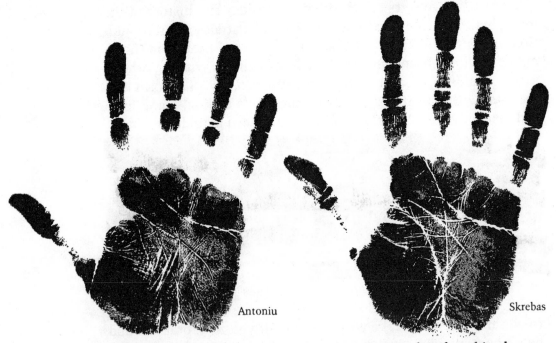

Antoniu

Skrebas

Half-brothers Kimon Antoniu and Sotiris Skrebas are also close friends. Note the similarity in the shape of their hands and in their heart lines. Both of them have emigrated from Greece; note that both life lines tend toward Luna.

he'd be expressing his love to you with the donation, but you can't put it in a vase on the living room table. It's interesting to experiment with different kinds of people, and it's possible to compromise and learn to accept the idiosyncrasies of our loved ones, but the compatibility factors are designed to help you increase the odds that your relationship will work. Since it's possible for each of us to find someone whose way of loving harmonizes with our own, we might as well focus on finding that sort of person from the start. The more factors you have in your favor from the beginning, the more likely your relationship is to be happy and nourishing for you both.

The more similar your heart lines are, the fewer drastic compromises you'll have to make. If you know that your heart line ending in Jupiter shows a great need for self-fulfillment and some possessiveness but you still feel magnetized to someone with a humanitarian heart line, you can still go for it. It might be worth the compromise. He might even get you a donation card that goes with your tablecloth.

Look at your own hands carefully before you ogle anyone else's. Is your heart line straight or chained? Where does it end? How did it all begin? What shape is your hand in? Do the interpretations of hand shape and heart line given previously fit your perception of yourself? If not, other factors in your hands may modify certain qualities or alter your attitudes about yourself. Regardless of these modifications, there is usually a basic attitude or set of beliefs which is conditioning the way you choose and behave in the major relationships of your life. See if you can observe what these beliefs are.

Suppose you are a man and you spot Ms. Wonderful at your next cocktail party. The strapless evening dress is great, the tan is impeccable, but *how about her heart line!* Tell her you're studying palmistry and she'll probably purr, "Oh, my, but what about mine?" If your hand shapes are different, but not too different, move on to the heart line. How does it look and where does it end?

If it's clear and unblemished, you've stumbled on a pearl of constant charm. You may be fickle, but never she. If it's chained, as most people's are, be patient. She's been disappointed often and she may find it hard to trust you. That does not mean she cannot love and it certainly doesn't mean she doesn't want to, only that it is hard for her to find a man to trust. (Can she trust you? If not, either tell her so at the start so she can make an informed decision or leave her alone.)

Next, examine the ending of her heart line and compare it with your own. If both of you have lines ending between Jupiter and Saturn, you're in luck. Both of you are balanced, and both of you are affectionate—now if only you can dance a decent rumba. If even one of you has the ending between Jupiter and Saturn, the relationship has a chance. If, however, your line is over on Jupiter and hers is up on Saturn, head back to the hors d'oeuvres table and try again. You won't want to be around when your possessiveness sets her perfectionist jaws in motion. The Compatibility Guide contains a list of all possible combinations of heart line endings, along with their significance. Use your intuition to make the information there come alive.

Thumb in Thumb

If your hand shape and heart line are fairly balanced, you have the beginnings of a sweet duet. If nothing else, you can be good friends. Having passed through the two essential areas, you move on to the three supporting factors, namely, the thumb, the Mount

Maynard and Chole Breslow have been married to—and divorced from— each other three times. We can see the compatibility between the heart lines and the Mounts of Venus, but note that the hand shapes are quite disimilar. Their duaghter, Susan, has hands more similar to her mother's.

Maynard Breslow

of Venus and the marriage line(s). The thumb is a compatibility factor because it gives an instant overview of how the person sees himself in relation to the rest of the world. If it's hunched over, he lacks confidence and tends to suppress his true desires. (A temporarily hunched thumb only shows that he's doing something he'd rather not be doing at that moment, but if talking to you is something he could live without, it's hors d'oeuvres time for you again.) A rigid thumb shows an unwillingness to compromise and a floppy thumb shows a spineless namby-pamby attitude. If you want a yes-man or a whipping boy, sign up here. But first examine yourself to see why relationships like that excite you.

If the thumb is graceful and proportionate, the person is capable of standing up for himself without being rigid. He is likely to keep his word. Two people with flexible thumbs make an ideal match, since the flexible thumb is equivalent to a heart line ending between Jupiter and Saturn. It shows an ability to adapt and compromise. Of course, other factors on the thumb such as its set, length, and the proportion between the two joints, reveal important aspects of the character, but from the point of view of relationships, it's how strongly the will is expressed that counts. That is, who cares if he's naturally stubborn as long as he's good to you?

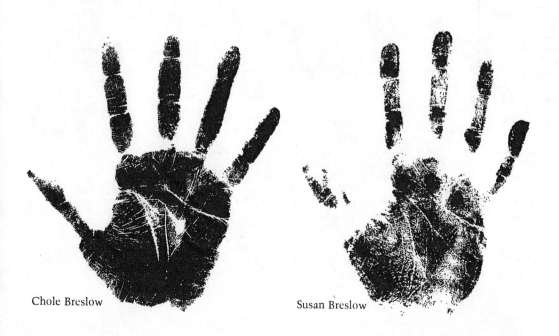

Chole Breslow   Susan Breslow

HAND IN HAND'S COMPATIBILITY GUIDE FOR
CO-WORKERS

HAND SHAPE
E Elementary
SQ Square
SP Spatulate
C Conic
P Pointed

	P	C	SP	SQ	E	
					Neither One Can Lead	**E**
				Excellent Team	Good Camaraderie	**SQ**
			Ego Conflict Likely	Start a Company	OK if Sp. Leads	**SP**
		Slow Starters	Good if Sp. Leads	Very Productive	Unlikely Match	**C**
	Will Probably Do Little	OK in Low-pressure Jobs	A Challenge	Forget It	Conflicting Styles	**P**

HEART LINE ENDINGS
X Crosses Completely
½ Ends Halfway
S Ends in Saturn
S/J Ends between Saturn and Jupiter
J Ends in Jupiter

	X	½	S	S/J	J	
X	Shared Goals					**E**
½	Good Working Relationship	Low Production				**SQ**
S	Difficult Communication	Tense	Nit-pickers Unite			**SP**
S/J	Good Balance	Very Fine	Tolerable	Excellent		**C**
J	A Little Uncomfortable	Potentially Frustrating	Be Patient with Each Other	Harmonious	Very Intense	**J**

(bottom labels: X   ½   S   S/J   J)

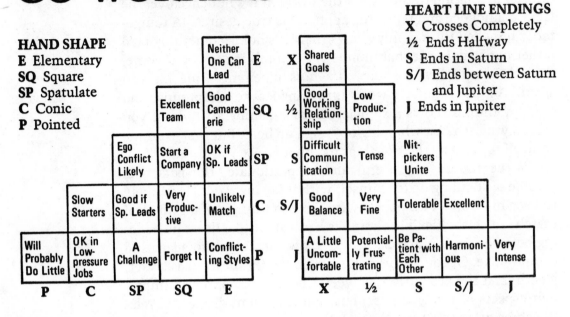

THUMB
R Rigid
FLX Flexible
FPY Floppy

	R	FLX	FLP
R	Locked Horns		
FLX	Negotiable	Ideal	
FLP	Dominant/Submissive	So-so	Low Productivity

MOUNT OF VENUS
H High
M Moderate
F Flat

	F	M	H	
			High Energy	**H**
		Steady Work	Excellent Balance	**M**
	Low Motivation	Fine for Routine Job	Frustration	**F**

MARRIAGE LINES

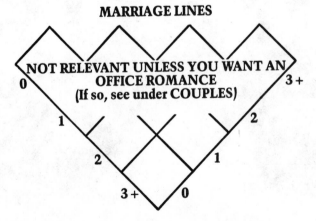

NOT RELEVANT UNLESS YOU WANT AN OFFICE ROMANCE
(If so, see under COUPLES)

0   3+   1   2   2   1   3+   0

HAND IN HAND'S COMPATIBILITY SCORING FOR
CO-WORKERS

To calculate your innate compatibility with a co-worker or a person you would like to have as a co-worker: Look at your own hand and determine its shape. Write your shape in the appropriate blank in the "Your Type" column. Write the shape of your co-worker's hand in the "Co-Worker's Type" column. On the large chart, opposite left, locate the square that is common to both types; you will get a clue as to the compatibility of your two hand shapes from the words in the square. That clue has a numerical value in the corresponding square in the small chart to the right. Write this number in the appropriate blank in the "Combined Factor Scores" column. Repeat this process with the other Compatibility Factors, taking special note of the first two factors—hand shape and heart line—as they are considered prerequisites for a good relationship. Add up the individual Combined Factor Scores to determine your Total Compatibility Score and check the key at the bottom of the page. Remember that the Compatibility Guide is simply a tool to help you focus your own intuitive sense of what is best for you.

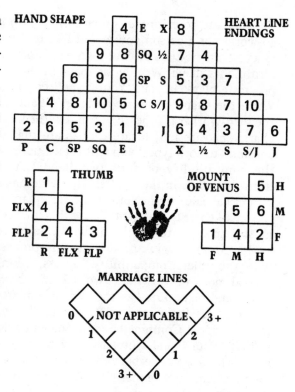

Compatibility Factor	Your Type	Co-Worker's Type	Combined Factor Score
Hand Shape	_____	_____	_____
Heart Line Ending	_____	_____	_____
Thumb	_____	_____	_____
Mount of Venus	_____	_____	_____
Marriage Lines	_____	_____	_____
		Total Compatibility Score:	_____

Key to Factor Scores
Hand Shape and Heart Line: 1 Forget it. **2** Take this job... **3** Blah. **4** So-so. **5** A fighting chance. **6** Why not? **7** A good bet. **8** Upbeat office. **9** Excellent mix. **10** Worker's paradise. **Thumb and Mt. of Venus: 1** Forget it. **2** Tepid. **3** Getting there. **4** Worth a try. **5** Looking good. **6** Excellent.

Key to Total Score
4–11 Get another job (or at least another colleague).
12–19 Do it if you must.
20–26 Enjoyable work.
27–32 Work is bliss.

HAND IN HAND'S COMPATIBILITY SCORING FOR
CO-WORKERS

To calculate your innate compatibility with a co-worker or a person you would like to have as a co-worker: Look at your own hand and determine its shape. Write your shape in the appropriate blank in the "Your Type" column. Write the shape of your co-worker's hand in the "Co-Worker's Type" column. On the large chart, opposite left, locate the square that is common to both types; you will get a clue as to the compatibility of your two hand shapes from the words in the square. That clue has a numerical value in the corresponding square in the small chart to the right. Write this number in the appropriate blank in the "Combined Factor Scores" column. Repeat this process with the other Compatibility Factors, taking special note of the first two factors—hand shape and heart line—as they are considered prerequisites for a good relationship. Add up the individual Combined Factor Scores to determine your Total Compatibility Score and check the key at the bottom of the page. Remember that the Compatibility Guide is simply a tool to help you focus your own intuitive sense of what is best for you.

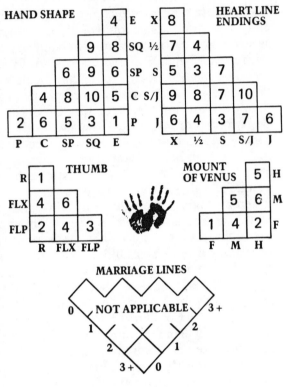

Compatibility Factor	Your Type	Co-Worker's Type	Combined Factor Score
Hand Shape	_____	_____	_____
Heart Line Ending	_____	_____	_____
Thumb	_____	_____	_____
Mount of Venus	_____	_____	_____
Marriage Lines	_____	_____	_____
	Total Compatibility Score:		_____

Key to Factor Scores
Hand Shape and Heart Line: 1 Forget it. 2 Take this job. . . 3 Blah. 4 So-so. 5 A fighting chance. 6 Why not? 7 A good bet. 8 Upbeat office. 9 Excellent mix. 10 Worker's paradise. **Thumb and Mt. of Venus:** 1 Forget it. 2 Tepid. 3 Getting there. 4 Worth a try. 5 Looking good. 6 Excellent.

Key to Total Score
4–11	Get another job (or at least another colleague).
12–19	Do it if you must.
20–26	Enjoyable work.
27–32	Work is bliss.

The Mount of Venus

The Mount of Venus is like a volcano. It can be live, dormant, or petrified. Your feelings about its condition will vary depending on what sort of relationship you want. As the storehouse of physical energy, it also indicates the force of a person's sexual drive and his appreciation for the sensual. If you're looking for romance, consider three factors when studying your prospect's mount: the size of the mount in proportion to the rest of the hand, the size of your own mount, and how you feel about the difference. If you're not looking for passion, let the Mount of Venus indicate the person's enthusiasm for life and his stamina. These qualities are also important in romantic relationships, but since physical passion is usually what distinguishes couples from friends, we'll focus here on sexual compatibility.

Suppose you are a woman just introduced to a gorgeous, husky man at a dinner party. Your hostess assures you he's Bruce Jenner and you believe her. He's not, but so what. He eyes you up and down and a slight sweat rapidly coats your body. You casually mention the book you're reading and leap for his hand. His hands are square and yours are conic: Perfect! His heart line ends between Jupiter and Saturn: Heaven! His thumb is even flexible. But alas. The Mount of Venus looks like Death Valley. As you talk it becomes clear that the great build came from steroids and weight-lifting, the voice came from a self-improvement course, and the repartee, though clever, sounds like it's coming from a game show host. Alas. The electricity is all yours. A wizened Mount of Venus is a sure sign that physical passion is not his long suit. Particularly if the Mount of Lower Mars (the "pillow" on the upper half of the Mount of Venus, closest to the thumb) is drained, his physical energy is just not oriented toward sex. So if sex is what you're looking for, keep looking. It does not mean that he never makes love, it's just that he's not likely to make it an art form. If you've abandoned painting and sculpture in favor of perfecting the arts of pleasure, then head for the spinach quiche again. If, however, your Mount of Venus is flattened, too, you can have a great time together. Talking.

Mounts of Venus should be of similar height and firmness to increase the likelihood that when you're hot, he's hot, too.

Marriage: Who'll Be the Next in Line?

Marriage lines indicate committed relationships. If you're not looking for a committed relationship, then you needn't consider the marriage lines at all. A flaming Mount of Venus might be enough. If marriage is your goal, however, scrutinize these lines before you wade into the relationship too deeply. A person can have more marriages than he has lines, but he can also have fewer marriages than he has lines. As in all other areas of the hands, the lines show probabilities, which are made into certainties by the person's commitment—and his destiny.

Unmarried relationships with "significant others" do appear as marriage lines. It's the intensity and commitment of the relationship that appears on the hand, not the marriage license.

When examining the lines of prospective partners, look at two factors: how many lines are there and what shape are they in? Only after answering these questions should you check out what kind of car the person drives. After you've seen how many marriage lines he has, inquire offhandedly about his marital history. So much time and effort can be saved by asking that little question, "Are you married?" right at the start. If he's already been married twice and he has but two marriage lines, then he may have had it with marriage. A third such bond would have to be created from pure intention and desire, since it's not yet written in his hands.

The condition of the marriage lines is also important since it tells you whether the person had strong marriages in the past and whether he is still upset about or involved in a previous relationship. If the first marriage line looks weak and frail and he tells you he is divorced, then you know that either he wasn't committed to that relationship from the start or he is not interested in it now. If the earlier marriage lines appear reddish or have white or dark spots on them, then he is still embroiled in the emotions of his previous relationships. His "ex" will always be with you, if not in body then in mind. Since he has not released the negativity of the past, he might be blocked in creating a new and positive relationship. You have three choices here: hang in there while he works it out, enjoy yourself with someone else while he works it out, or bless him and wish him the best as you trust that you will meet the appropriate person at just the right time, as will he. In love as in winemaking, timing is everything.

David Brenner

Joy Brenner

An excellent marriage. In the hands of David and Joy Brenner, notice that her hand is more conical and his is more square, and that their heart lines are also quite compatible.

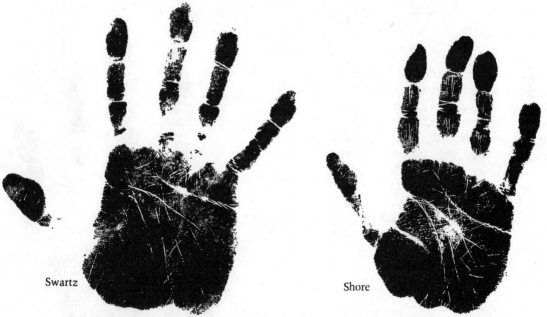

Swartz

Shore

Jerram Swartz and Debbie Shore are another couple who both live and work together. Once again, both hands have a spatulate tone, although Debbie's hand is also conic and Jerram's is a bit square. The heart lines are a bit dissimilar, but not enough to break the bond between the two characters.

Hand in Hand

These, then, are the general interpretations of the five compatibility factors in the hands. All possible combinations of these factors are listed in the Compatibility Guides along with a system for scoring them. Don't be rigid in your assessment of the factors (remember that someone can have a hand that is partly square and partly conic); and be lenient with the people you like. The five factors are like the five fingers of the hand. Each one tells you something valuable and specific about the character, yet all of them have the same base. The base is the person himself, in all his complexity and beauty.

Look at your own hands so that you know what your scores are. Think about what you'd like to see in the hands of a new lover. What kind of heart line would he or she have? What shape would the hands be? How high would you like the Mount of Venus? Don't think of cultural stereotypes here, rather, imagine the sort of person who would balance *you*, someone whose love *you'd* care to share. Some people look great on billboards, but you might not enjoy waking up next to them. Think about what's best for yourself.

Donna David-Langer and Stu Langer are relationships consultants focusing on improving the quality of relationships as a way to enhance quality of life and natural productivity. Both of their hands are basically spatulate, and their heart lines are similar, too. This shows how they can be compatible coworkers as well as lovers. Stu's son, Scott, has a hand shape similar to his father's, although there is a stronger emphasis on the energies of Venus and Luna.

Stu Langer

Now imagine some of the hands that you think you'd be happy working with as employers and as subordinates. How do these hands differ from the hands of your Romeo or your Juliet? Notice the hands of your friends and think about how their hands reflect the things you love and hate about them. Can you see from your hands what personality traits drew you together?

True, everyone contains the spark of Divine Love, yet within the Divine falls the realm of personality. It is in the world of personality that compatibility palmistry is a boon. It helps you choose your companions. Just because you recognize someone as one embodiment of Divine Love doesn't mean you have to have dinner with him. Dogs and plants are embodiments of Divine Love, too, and you don't have dinner with them. Even after you're able to see God in everyone, there are some people you want to spend time with and some you don't. This is perfectly appropriate, since with more than three billion people on the planet you'd be pretty busy if you felt obliged to go out with all of them. Hands speak louder than words, so listen to them before you give out your phone number.

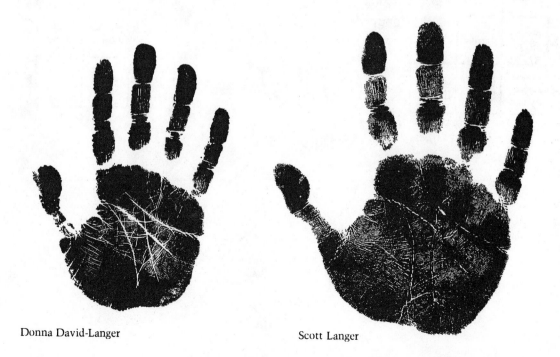

Donna David-Langer

Scott Langer

HAND IN HAND'S COMPATIBILITY GUIDE FOR
COUPLES

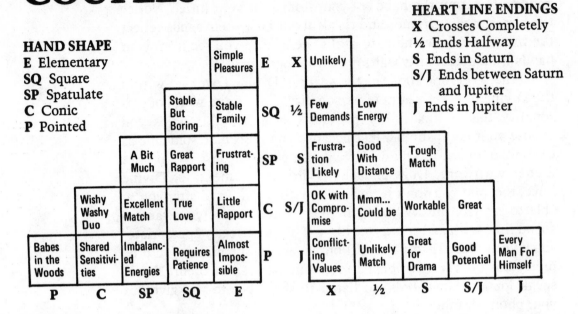

HAND SHAPE
- **E** Elementary
- **SQ** Square
- **SP** Spatulate
- **C** Conic
- **P** Pointed

	P	C	SP	SQ	E
E					Simple Pleasures
SQ				Stable But Boring	Stable Family
SP			A Bit Much	Great Rapport	Frustrating
C		Wishy Washy Duo	Excellent Match	True Love	Little Rapport
P	Babes in the Woods	Shared Sensitivities	Imbalanced Energies	Requires Patience	Almost Impossible

HEART LINE ENDINGS
- **X** Crosses Completely
- **½** Ends Halfway
- **S** Ends in Saturn
- **S/J** Ends between Saturn and Jupiter
- **J** Ends in Jupiter

	X	½	S	S/J	J
X	Unlikely				
½	Few Demands	Low Energy			
S	Frustration Likely	Good With Distance	Tough Match		
S/J	OK with Compromise	Mmm... Could be	Workable	Great	
J	Conflicting Values	Unlikely Match	Great for Drama	Good Potential	Every Man For Himself

THUMB
- **R** Rigid
- **FLX** Flexible
- **FPY** Floppy

	R	FLX	FLP
R	No Compromise		
FLX	Worth a Try	Terrific	
FLP	Unfair Power Balance	Could be Fun	Nothing Doing

MOUNT OF VENUS
- **H** High
- **M** Moderate
- **F** Flat

	F	M	H
H			Hot Times
M		Satisfactory	Good Balance
F	OK if you Have a Good TV	Quiet	Frustration

MARRIAGE LINES

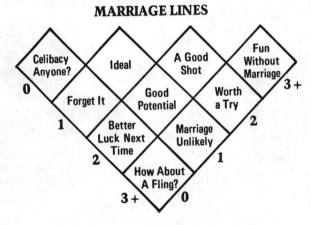

Celibacy Anyone? — Ideal — A Good Shot — Fun Without Marriage

Forget It — Good Potential — Worth a Try

Better Luck Next Time — Marriage Unlikely

How About A Fling?

0, 1, 2, 3+ / 3+, 2, 1, 0

114

HAND IN HAND'S COMPATIBILITY SCORING FOR
COUPLES

To calculate your innate compatibility with a lover or a person you would like to have as a lover: Look at your own hand and determine its shape. Write your shape in the appropriate blank in the "Your Type" column. Write the shape of your lover's hand in the "Lover's Type" column. On the large chart, opposite left, locate the square that is common to both types; you will get a clue as to the compatibility of your two hand shapes from the words in the square. That clue has a numerical value in the corresponding square in the small chart to the right. Write this number in the appropriate blank in the "Combined Factor Scores" column. Repeat this process with the other Compatibility Factors, taking special note of the first two factors—hand shape and heart line—as they are considered prerequisites for a good relationship. Add up the individual Combined Factor Scores to determine your Total Compatibility Score and check the key at the bottom of the page. Remember that the Compatibility Guide is simply a tool to help you focus your own intuitive sense of what is best for you.

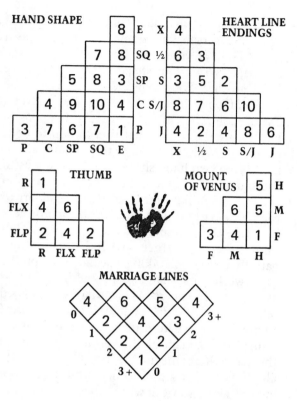

Compatibility Factor	Your Type	Lover's Type	Combined Factor Score
Hand Shape	_____	_____	_____
Heart Line Ending	_____	_____	_____
Thumb	_____	_____	_____
Mount of Venus	_____	_____	_____
Marriage Lines	_____	_____	_____
		Total Compatibility Score:	_____

Key to Factor Scores
Hand Shape and Heart Line: 1 Heartbreak House. **2** Forget it. **3** Blah. **4** Maybe. **5** The turning point. **6** Looks better. **7** Now you're talking. **8** Good. **9** Very good. **10** Heaven.
Thumb, Mt. of Venus and Marriage Lines: 1 Forget it. **2** Tepid. **3** Getting there. **4** Worth a try. **5** Looks good. **6** Fantastic.

Key to Total Scores
4–11	Keep looking.
12–19	An uphill march.
20–26	Changeable love.
27–32	A good match.
33–38	Bingo! True love.

HAND IN HAND'S COMPATIBILITY SCORING FOR
COUPLES

To calculate your innate compatibility with a lover or a person you would like to have as a lover: Look at your own hand and determine its shape. Write your shape in the appropriate blank in the "Your Type" column. Write the shape of your lover's hand in the "Lover's Type" column. On the large chart, opposite left, locate the square that is common to both types; you will get a clue as to the compatibility of your two hand shapes from the words in the square. That clue has a numerical value in the corresponding square in the small chart to the right. Write this number in the appropriate blank in the "Combined Factor Scores" column. Repeat this process with the other Compatibility Factors, taking special note of the first two factors—hand shape and heart line—as they are considered prerequisites for a good relationship. Add up the individual Combined Factor Scores to determine your Total Compatibility Score and check the key at the bottom of the page. Remember that the Compatibility Guide is simply a tool to help you focus your own intuitive sense of what is best for you.

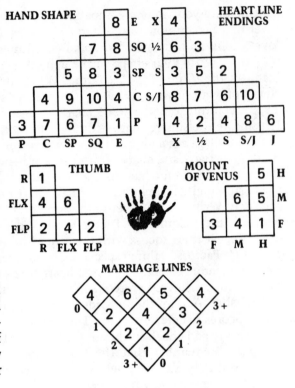

Compatibility Factor	Your Type	Lover's Type	Combined Factor Score
Hand Shape	_____	_____	_____
Heart Line Ending	_____	_____	_____
Thumb	_____	_____	_____
Mount of Venus	_____	_____	_____
Marriage Lines	_____	_____	_____
Total Compatibility Score:			_____

Key to Factor Scores
Hand Shape and Heart Line: 1 Heartbreak House. **2** Forget it. **3** Blah. **4** Maybe. **5** The turning point. **6** Looks better. **7** Now you're talking. **8** Good. **9** Very good. **10** Heaven.
Thumb, Mt. of Venus and Marriage Lines: 1 Forget it. **2** Tepid. **3** Getting there. **4** Worth a try. **5** Looks good. **6** Fantastic.

Key to Total Scores
4–11	Keep looking.
12–19	An uphill march.
20–26	Changeable love.
27–32	A good match.
33–38	Bingo! True love.

Shahastra   Zubin

Shahastra and Zubin are another "ideal match." His hands are spatulate and hers are conic, and both have heart lines ending between Saturn and Jupiter. Beautiful people!

When Compatibility Palmistry Does Not Work

The Compatibility Guide is useless for people who are not looking for compatibility. All of us know couples who claw at one another constantly, yet never break up. We've also seen couples who live together for years, sometimes decades, in deathlike stillness. Bored, resentful, yet afraid of change, they tense continually into rigidity and anger until dissolution and death claim their remains. These people know that they are miserable, yet if asked why they put up with it, they might answer, "It could be worse," or "I'm used to it," or "It's better than being alone," and so forth. To the rational mind, these couples are incompatible, yet to themselves and in practice they are compatible because they never part.

If you suspect that the person(s) you are reading for are "compatibly incompatible," notice it, but don't play along with the idea that their miseries are caused by God, the Federal Government, or the stars. They were created by and agreed to by everyone involved, and everyone involved perpetuates them by continually renewing their agreement to have them. Their lives together are a joint production, like a home movie. If someone claims that he has nothing to do with the circumstances of his life, then he's forgotten that his life is *his* movie and no one else's. Don't you forget, too. Point out the strong points and the weak points of the relationship as you see it and encourage each person to take responsibility for himself. Probably neither of them will, but once they sense that you're in a different movie than theirs, they'll find another theater. Also, remember that in a few moments of looking at their hands, you cannot see the awesome network of shared moments, beliefs, dreams and fears that have brought and kept these two together. Who knows, they may own lakefront property together. You can see the basic themes of the relationship, so share this and let them be.

There's a point at which, no matter how tempting it is to convert people to our ideas of happiness, we have to accept them as manifesting God exactly as they are. If they want to manifest God in the form of misery, that's their business.

Using Compatibility Palmistry For Your Own Happiness

Whenever you deal with other people, compatibility palmistry works to your advantage. You can use it to check out the hands of a prospective employer. Does she hold her thumb rigidly? Then your ideas for eliminating the time clock will be punched out. You can use it in your personal business. If you need the house painted in midsummer and two painters apply, one who has pointed hands and one who has square hands, which one is more likely to complete the job with the fewest lemonade breaks in the shortest time? The square hand. The pointy-hander is more likely to fall off the ladder in a swoon. However, if you need your Rembrandt restored, trust the sensitive hands of Mr. Pointy.

Compatibility palmistry is also useful in helping us distinguish between whim and intuitive knowledge. The intuitive mind always tells us the truth, but we don't always like the truth, so we sometimes deceive ourselves. Although your intuition will guide you in selecting the lucky people who share your time, it's possible to err in identifying an intuitive flash. Great credence has been given in our day to vague thoughts and feelings, but these "feelings" are not always the product of our true intuitive mind. Sometimes they come from childish or unconscious thought patterns. In doubtful cases, compatibility palmistry can be particularly helpful, since it is an accurate way to confirm intuitive feelings.

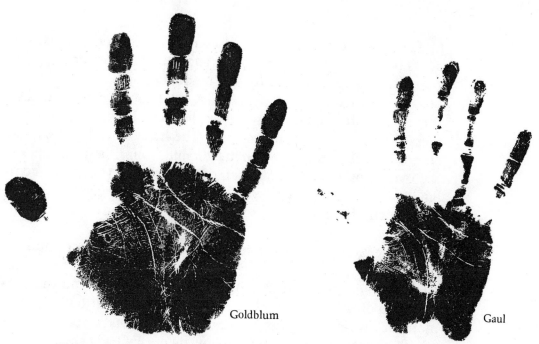

Goldblum

Gaul

Television, stage, and movie actor Jeff Goldblum and his actress wife, Patricia Gaul, have a close marriage. Their hands show an interesting balance between the spatulate and the pointed, and their heart lines are perfectly matched.

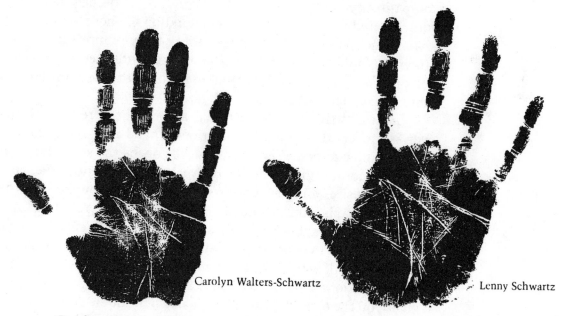

Carolyn Walters-Schwartz

Lenny Schwartz

Carolyn Walters-Schwartz and Lenny Schwartz have a strong marriage. The hand shapes are similar, but not too similar. Both heart lines end between Saturn and Jupiter. Even the head lines complement each other. Their hands show that they are friends as well as lovers.

Most of us are tempted at times to buy shirts that don't look good on us because they're designed by someone famous, or to get involved with someone who doesn't nourish us because they look or talk a certain way. Some people act a lot more wonderful than they really are, and even sensitive people like us can be hard-pressed to discern this at the start. The hands loyally reflect the character of their owner. With insight and compassion you can see the overall patterns and character of the people you meet, combine this awareness with your awareness of yourself and your desires, and have a clearer sense of how to nurture the relationship.

Make palmistry your friend, and allow it to open communication between you and those who interest you. On that first date, when the silence between soup and entrée drags on and the conversation of the people at the next table ceases to titillate, in that moment, whip out your palms. Within seconds you can tell whether that silence is due to the magic of two lovers discovering each other or if your roommate was right when she said you'd be better off with Bonzo.

If you know what your desires and tolerances are, you can use compatibility palmistry to get an overview of the new people in your life and to deepen your understanding of those you already love. Remember that, over time, variety is more interesting than sameness, so don't be put off if someone is different from you. Look for differences that turn you on in the context of similarities that make you feel at home.

Greater than the informational aspect of the reading, however, is the fact that holding your friend's hand and talking to him about his character and emotional needs opens the space for both of you to communicate more freely about your true selves and your true desires and expectations. It gives you a low-key setting in which to air your thoughts and fears about relationships. Everyone has thoughts and fears about closeness, except maybe a few saints, and the sooner you air your resistance the sooner it will disappear. If you both maintain your social facades indefinitely, your relationship will be a facade. Sharing palmreadings is fun, it gives you the opportunity to hold hands without seeming pushy, and it gives you real insight into the lives of those who are close to you or with whom you want to be close. So move over, relax and hold that hand. Are you hand in hand with love?

7

AWARENESS

In addition to telling us whether things are hot or cold, hard or soft, and smooth or prickly, our hands contribute to our awareness in a variety of ways. The study of the lines, marks, mounts and other features of the hands gives us more insight into our talents and the trends of our lives. An additional, and potentially more significant way in which the hands contribute to our awareness is this. By focusing on reading the hands we focus our minds. You cannot read the hands without concentrating on them carefully. This mental concentration is a greater tool than palmistry itself.

When you know how to read the hands, you learn about yourself and others, but only while you are looking at the hands. When you know how to calm and focus your mind, you learn more and feel better *all* the time. Beginning from awareness of the hands, we will now move on to new levels of awareness in which everything we do becomes a form of meditation, and everything we see reveals itself as a form of universal energy. With practice, you will come to see the flurry of activity around you as a cosmic dance in which basic life energy manifests itself in myriad forms. There is no separation between the essence of one thing and the essence of another. Apparent divisons are produced by the dance of indefatigable life which creates them for drama and fun. You will learn how to create a drama that you like, so that your life will never again seem like a movie that you'd like to walk out on.

By developing increased awareness, you become able to read the hands—and much, much more. You can learn to be more *self-aware*, and the more you practice this the more adept you will become. We will begin with a few energy awareness exercises which relate specifically to the hands, and then move on to awareness exercises for the body, mind, and spirit. The first three exercises are basic. They are the Golden Ball, the Neighbor's Field, and the Energy Circle.

Follow the Golden Ball

Your body is bathed in a field of energy which is sometimes called the "aura." You can feel this aura more strongly as your self-awareness increases. The process of becoming more aware of your energy begins right between your own hands.

Sit comfortably in a room of average temperature. Hold your hands close together, but not touching. (Pretend they're on their first date.) Feel the warmth between them. Slowly begin to move your hands apart, continuing to feel the warmth. When they are about six inches apart, imagine that the warmth between them has become a golden ball. Play with the ball, shifting it from side to side or moving your hands wider apart to make the ball bigger. It's your ball—you can expand it to take up the whole room or scrunch it down to nothing. You can pull it apart like salt water taffy or dribble it across the living room like a basketball. Feel the heat between your hands. Feel it expand and contract. Enjoy playing with this ball of energy which you have created between your hands.

If you don't feel the energy between your hands right away, that's fine. Rub them together briskly until they warm up and hold them close together to feel the heat. Move your hands apart and let the ball grow. If you rub your hands together and you still don't feel any heat, that's fine, too. The room may be too cold for you or the Golden Ball may have taken time-out. Try again another time. Eventually the exercise will work for you.

Your Neighbor's Field

Once you learn to feel the energy in your own hands, you can begin to explore the energy in the hands of others. The Neighbor's

Field exercise is like the Golden Ball exercise, except that two people do it together.

Sit comfortably facing your friend. Each of you hold your hands up with the palms facing out, as though you were about to play pattycake. Imagine a warm flow of energy traveling through your arms and into your hands, making them warm and light. Ask your friend to fill his hands with warmth, too. Move your hands toward each other, still without touching, until both of you feel the warmth between you. After a few minutes of enjoying this energy connection, slowly lower your hands.

Neighbor's Field

Will the Circle Be Unbroken?

This exercise will prepare you to do "psychic palmreading." Its form is simple. You hold hands with a friend and feel the energy circulate between you. Despite its simplicity, this exercise can produce profound results. In order to assure that you get the best possible results from doing this exercise, a few preparatory measures are recommended.

Sit quietly facing your friend. Sit up straight, uncross your arms and legs, and take several deep breaths. Imagine a pyramid of white light surrounding your body, its top directly above your head and its four points touching the ground around you on all four sides. See this as clearly as you can in your mind's eye. You are the only inhabitant of this particular pyramid.

Feel your hips sink into the chair, making you conscious of gravity pulling you steadily toward the center of the earth. Put your attention in your navel center, which is located about three inches below your navel. (This is your center of gravity.) Imagine this area becoming warm. Feel it contract sightly as it sends the warmth straight up into your heart center, located at the center of your chest. Feel the heart area grow warm. Now imagine the warmth traveling up to the third eye point, located on the forehead directly between the eyes. Feel this area become warm.

These preliminary exercises are designed to stabilize you in your own energy field before you link up with anyone else's. After you've completed your preparations, take your partner's hands.

The exercise itself is easy. Hold your friend's hands, relax, and listen. Put your attention in your own hands and feel where your hands touch his. If your hands move spontaneously to feel your friend's hands, let them. Concentrate on feeling the circulation of energy between your hands. Notice any energy pulsations, changes in temperature, or other perceptions about the person and his hands, and enjoy the opportunity you have to learn more about your friend. You will probably find that you and your friend draw your hands apart at about the same time. Pause for a moment with your hands in your lap and center yourself again before you stand up.

By practicing the Golden Ball, the Neighbor's Field, and the Energy Circulation exercises you will increase your awareness of energy flows in the hands.

Your Body: Love It or Leave It

Starting from awareness of the hands, you can expand into awareness of other parts of your body. You might even start a dialogue with your big toe. Since all the major experiences of our lives happen in and around our bodies, they're good things to be aware of. You can begin to expand your awareness by noticing your body right now. Where are you? Are you comfortable? Warm, damp, or cold? How are you sitting? Is your back straight, or are you auditioning to be the Hunchback of Notre Dame? Are there any tense spots in your body? Where are they? Feel your feet flat on the floor. How much weight is on them? Without mental critique, be conscious of your body right now.

Many of us avoid looking at and feeling our bodies because we're afraid of what we might find there. There could be tensions, pains, stored up anxieties, maybe even guppies, that we'd rather not acknowledge. What we don't realize is that by not looking at our tensions, we keep them there. Next time you feel a pain, put your attention *into* it rather than try to avoid it. Observe it as if you wanted to describe it in the minutest detail. For example, you could say, "There is a three inch by two inch by four inch area in the left side of my abdomen which feels like the entire U.S. Army is walking over it in cleats." That's specific. You might be amazed at the results. Just looking at our pains often makes them disappear.

Developing body awareness does not mean prancing naked in front of a mirror all day. It means staying attuned to the internal and external changes in our bodies. It also means accepting that we are going to live in our bodies all our lives, and agreeing to be conscious of them and take care of them. Many of us act as though our bodies were $7 per night motel rooms rather than places we intend to inhabit for a while. If you own a house and you plan to stay there several years, you're likely to keep a close eye on the plumbing. Why not give your body the same good care?

Body Awareness Exercise

Here's a basic exercise you can do to relax and increase your awareness of your body.

> Lie comfortably on your back with your clothing loosened so that your breathing is not restricted. Breathe deeply several times, inhaling until your lungs fill your whole chest and exhaling until they feel as small as split peas.

> Put your attention in your feet. Don't think about them, *feel* them, right down there at the end of your body. Feel the toes and the arches and the heels. Be conscious of your *feet* and feel them become warm. Let the warmth seep up into your *ankles, calves and knees.* Don't rush it, just let the heat slide up. Then let the heat rise into your *thighs,* filling them with light and strength. Feel the bones and muscles of your thighs become warm. Let the warmth glide up into your *genitals and pelvis.* Feel light and warmth permeate all the organs and bones in this area.

> Next, let the warmth rise up through your eliminative and digestive systems, including the *kidneys, bladder and colon.* Feel these organs. How are they? Ask them if there's anything they'd like you to know about their condition and your general health. Listen to them, bless them and move on. Let the warmth enter the center of your abdomen, bathing the *small intestine, liver, pancreas, gall bladder and spleen* with healing light. (It's okay if you don't know exactly where these organs are: They know where they are. Call their names and ask for messages and they'll be there to support you.) Feel the

warmth enter your *stomach and esophagus*. Feel them relax as you let them speak to you. If your stomach says, ''No more chili,'' you'd be wise to listen. When we ignore the subtle messages from our bodies they make sure we get the message by making us sick. So listen carefully; esophagi need love, too.

Next, feel the warmth enter your *heart and lungs*, expanding and relaxing them with nourishing light.

Feel all your organs purring harmoniously inside you as the blood flows smoothly through all your cells, bringing them nourishment and light. Look inside your body. Feel it, listen to it. It is where you live. Notice that it's cheaper than a condominium if you maintain it right.

Let the warmth rise and fill your body with conscious love as it moves up into your *neck and throat*. It travels smoothly down your *arms* and then vitalizes your *hands and each of your fingers*. Then it flows back up into your *face and head*. Feel your face soften and relax as the warmth enters every cell. As the warmth enters your head, look at your brain. It's the squishy-looking thing with all the wrinkles. Let the warmth fill the front, the back and both sides of your brain. Notice any differences between the right and left sides. Let the light of conscious awareness bathe your noggin, opening it and expanding its circulation.

Look back over your body from toes to temples and notice what an awesome and beautiful creation it is. Even if there are blockages or sick spots, or if you think your nose is too big or your mouth is too small, even if parts of it are missing, it still *works*. Something must be working or you wouldn't be able to think about whether it works. You are alive, in your body, experiencing Universal Energy in all its playful forms. Enjoy it.

During this exercise you might find some spots where the flow of warmth bogs down. These might appear as dark spots or muddy areas in your visualization. Observe these areas closely but dispassionately, and do not try to explain them. If you listen close-ly enough, they will explain themselves to you. Watch them, pro-ject a little more light into them and move on.

Notice the sense of well-being that grows in you from simply breathing into the warmth and the light. Also notice that this is cheaper than drugs, alcohol or psychotherapy—and faster, too. You have added nothing but breath and focused awareness, yet your energy level has almost certainly increased. Many of us think that we need more energy when in fact, we are the energy factory.

Knowing Your Own Mind

Awareness of the body is closely linked to awareness of the mind. It seems as though it's the job of the mind to be aware, so it's re-dundant to speak of "being aware of the mind." Who is aware of the mind if not the mind itself? If you reflect on your own experi-ence, however, you'll see that you can in fact be aware of the con-tents of your own mind. What are you thinking now? How do you know? There is a part of us, however, which is neither our mind, nor our emotions, nor our body. This is the witness, or inner self. It is steadily serene. It observes the shenanigans of mind, heart and body and is unscathed by the upsets of daily life. This is the part of us that is always on center, always alert, and always in communion with universal energy. It is the universal energy within us, the cosmic referee.

Indian sages call this the *witness* of the mind, or the True or Absolute Self. It is the "me" referred to in phrases such as "my mind" or "my body." This aspect of us is conscious of its unity with all other beings. When we become more attuned to it, our perspective broadens, and we see the luminous consciousness within us which is beyond the flux of our thoughts, feelings and tummyaches. Our minds and hearts may run wild, but the True Self stays cool, because it sees the whole picture, not just the little corner where we got a flat tire in the middle of rush hour. As our self-awareness grows, we feel more and more the calming pres-ence of the true self.

Being aware of our minds means knowing *what* we are think-ing *when* we are thinking it. This is trickier than it sounds. The same thoughts usually run around our minds like a pack of fieldmice, conditioning our perceptions and forming the basis of our daily experience. Like fieldmice, these gnawing little thoughts scoot away as soon as we turn a flashlight on them. Looking at them makes them disappear.

Relationships, jobs, health conditions and other elements of our lives occur as a result of our attitudes, thoughts and beliefs. When we are aware of our own thoughts we have more influence over them, and we can alter them to create the experiences we desire. When we refuse to acknowledge thoughts which already exist inside of us, we drive them underground. Since they are not brought out in a way that we can look at and discard them if we no longer want them, they find expression in other ways. Repressed thoughts create depression, anger, and sickness, and draw to us the very experiences which we try hardest to resist. All that these renegade thoughts want from us is acknowledgement; when we are willing to accept their existence they lose their destructive grip on our lives. The more conscious we become of our unexamined thoughts and beliefs, the more choice we have in the quality of our lives.

In addition to hidden beliefs, mental chatter also contributes to our lack of awareness of our own minds. Random thoughts run roughshod through our minds, wasting time and energy. Although our prattle may fall into categories such as "sex" or "money" or "the Dodgers," it is basically content-free. The only thing it produces is more of itself. It creates anxiety and confusion where there could be calm. The Buddhists call this part of ourselves the "monkey mind" because it constantly chatters and jumps around. Does your mind steal peanuts, too?

When we flutter between unexamined beliefs and mental gossip, we lose one of our most precious assets: a stable, focused mind. Problems solve themselves when we are thinking clearly, but how often do most of us think clearly? (Let's see now, I think it was, no maybe it was . . .) The irony is that we have not really lost the quiet mind. We forgot about it. We do not need to seek peace of mind; all we need to do is stop avoiding it.

The best way to regain our natural clarity is to stay watchful of physical, mental and emotional sensations. We need not suppress them, because if we do they'll snap back and bite us. But we also need not egg them on. If we stay conscious of ourselves and of the changes within us, appropriate action will be self-evident.

Due to the essential identity of body sensations, thoughts, and motions, enhanced awareness in one of these areas automatically leads to enhanced awareness in the others. We will use three tools to encourage greater awareness—The Pause Button, Troubles the Clown, and meditation. Meditation can take you far beyond awareness of body, mind and heart into a vision of the unity of these three aspects, and it is of such importance it will have a chapter to itself later on. Right now we will get acquainted with the Pause Button and Troubles the Clown.

The Pause Button

Many tape recorders have a pause button, which enables you to temporarily stop recording while leaving the power on. It's the tape recorder's equivalent of a time-out, and it lets you stop for a moment and look at what you're doing before you play the whole tape. You have a pause button inside of you, and you can press it any time. It's easy to use. Just catch yourself in the middle of a thought, speech or action, and notice what you are doing without rationalizing or self-criticism. This is your time-out for self-awareness, which helps you stop and say, "What am I doing?" or "Why am I doing (or saying) this?" It provides a moment of clear observation in the midst of the fireworks in the mind.

Unfortunately, we are most likely to forget about the Pause Button just when we need it most. If we were always self-aware, we wouldn't have to press the button. The fact remains, however, that most of us do pop in and out of self-awareness, so the Pause Button is extremely helpful.

The Pause Button has two major functions. It halts an unbridled flow of thoughts and emotions and it prevents us from acting in haste. When any of us hit on a really juicy train of endlessly repetitive thought, we are no longer aware that we are thinking. We drone on, so absorbed in next week's party or last week's quarrel that we hardly know where we are. Nevertheless, the constant repetition of our thoughts is conditioning our experience in the most powerful way.

You can see this syndrome clearly by watching drivers in their cars, especially drivers who are alone. Some of them are tapping the steering wheel to the sound of rock and roll, others are speeding blindly, afraid of being late, some are crying, some are laughing, and others are talking to themselves or to some invisible second party. Many of them seem dull and hard, as though they were coated with emotional shellac. All of them are just driving cars, yet it is rare indeed to find anyone who knows he is doing only that. If any of these spellbound drivers would press their Pause Buttons, they would suddenly realize, "Hey! I'm upset at Harold and he's not here." or "My freeway exit was two miles back." Catching ourselves in the act of being functionally asleep enables us to stay awake more and more of the time.

The Pause Button also helps us to think before we act. "Act in haste, repent at leisure," says the proverb, and so it is. How often we have rushed to say something or do something or go somewhere fast, only to rue the impulse moments later. Some impulses are legitimate products of the accurate intuitive mind, but snap decisions can also come from fear, habit and abiding lack of perspective. A moment's clear reflection usually tells us whether our impulse has come from the true self or the monkey mind. Press your Pause Button *before* you act—don't wait for the consequences of your haste to slam you in the face.

You can decide now to use your Pause Button regularly. Start your own Candid Camera show. Right in the middle of a dramatic showdown or an exotic stream of consciousness, stop and say to yourself, "Smile! You're on Candid Camera!" How do you look? It's not that hard to keep an eye on ourselves once we affirm our intention to do so. Use the Pause Button to regain perspective when your monkey mind goes ape. It's inside you right now, waiting to be pressed. Smile!

Troubles the Clown

One morning I was standing before my bathroom mirror, brushing my hair and thinking about how wrong I was. Rivers of thoughts about my mistakes, my shortcomings and flaws spun through my mind as I stood there making my hair beautiful. I had called one person too early and another one too late, this part of me was too strong and that part was too weak. Whatever I was, was wrong. My wrongness seemed so right that I was unaware that I was playing a "tape loop" or repetitive pattern of negative thought. Suddenly the Pause Button went on and I saw myself standing there reciting my flaws. My mind flashed, "What would I do for entertainment if I wasn't making myself wrong?" I laughed. I had never realized what an important part of my entertainment agenda self-criticism had become.

Often we can relieve ourselves of the heaviness of our distress by seeing the absurdity and humor in it. Although this is sometimes hard, it's always possible to distance ourselves slightly from our situation and to see it as drama. The instant we begin to consciously enjoy the show, our burdens lift. It's easy to fall into the idea that some of the things that happen to us are right and others are wrong, and that it's good to be right and bad to be wrong. Most of us were raised with these dichotomies: good and bad, right and wrong, the Lone Ranger and the Indians. And we all know that it's *better* to be right, good, and the Lone Ranger. (Why else would he win every week?) Unfortunately, this belief in the superiority of being right numbs our ability to savor life, because life involves being wrong. If we were never wrong, we'd never learn anything, and we'd never get anything right. In fact, the opportunity to make mistakes and be wrong is one of the greatest educational tools around. When we make ourselves feel wrong for being wrong, however, we just feel worse and worse. Unwillingness to be wrong is a great barrier to growth.

There is another way to look at our feelings about right and wrong. Instead of thinking of ourselves in linear terms of good and bad or right and wrong, we can think of ourselves as expanding and contracting. Physically, mentally, and emotionally, each of us contains elements of expansion and contraction which create a natural syncopation. When we feel good, we are "expanded" (and expansive). When we feel bad, we are "contracted" and small. When we make what we think is a mistake, we don't really know if it will ultimately produce expansion (growth) or contraction (slowing down), but if we get upset about it we push ourselves unequivocally into contraction. We feel smaller, more defensive, more upset and more wrong. Although the force of contraction is not bad in itself, in excess it creates feelings of tension, limitation, and smallness. Yuck.

Have you ever noticed that trying to push something away brings it closer to you? That kicking the dog makes it want to bite you and that yelling at the child doesn't make her shut up? Have you noticed that if you ever say, "This will *never* happen to me," or "I will *never* do that," the things you forswore seem to be magnetized to you immediately? Resisting things makes them persist, and accepting them makes them pass away. Body surfers know this well. When a wall of water is about to pound you into the sand, there's only one thing to do—dive into it. The wave breaks on the beach and you surface in the gentle water behind the breakers.

Contraction makes us smaller, denser, and more resistant to change. Some contraction is necessary, but most of us overdo it, especially when we're hurt. Like potato bugs, we curl up at the first threat of attack and wait for the monsters to pass. Unfortunately, it doesn't help. Has it ever kept you from stomping on a bug? Has it ever made you believe the bug wasn't there? Of course not. All it did was tell you that the bug was scared to death. Emotionally, contraction takes the forms of anger, fear, defense mechanisms, sickness, and depression. It does us about as much good as it does the potato bug.

The only way to get out of contraction is by adding expansion. When we are upset (and we get upset because we're upset) we add contraction to contraction. When we're upset and we accept that we're upset, we add a little expansion. When we loosen our grip on our personal drama and *love* ourselves and our situations exactly as they are, we add a lot of expansion. Acceptance, awareness and love projected into the worst of apparent circumstances begin to bring back the light. You don't need a reason to love—the pleasure of loving is a reason in itself. Particularly when you feel like playing potato bug—love it the way it is. Love restores the music.

After acknowledging and experiencing the emotions associated with our drama, we can begin to watch the show for the sheer pleasure of watching. We can cry out, "Bravo! Author!" for the scenes we create and we can enjoy the convolutions of the plot. When we pour in positivity, contraction melts. Conflicts resolve themselves and appropriate action occurs. All we need to do is lighten up.

By pressing the Pause Button, we acknowledge what is happening, and this is often enough to renew our perspective and put us on center again. If you notice that you still feel contracted, resistant, or afraid, play the Troubles Game. Appreciate the drama in your situation and congratulate yourself on being both author and star. If you think you've done something wrong, pretend you're Johnny Carson and Ed McMahon—call out to yourself, "How wrong *were* you, _____?" And answer, "I was *so wrong* that . . ." and make up the most outrageous reply you can. Pretend that your life is a traveling circus in which one of the attractions is Troubles the Clown. He runs across the stage as part of the show, and then he runs off again. As long as you keep cheering, you'll have a good time, and the show can go on.

Awareness of your body, mind, and emotions will do more to simplify your life than anything else in the world. Although there are moments when it is uncomfortable or embarrassing to see the things we have said and done, nothing is more wasteful than spending our lives in a haze because we are unwilling to *look* at the things we have said and done. Nothing is more constricting than the avoidance of new experiences because of the possibility that the future will be like the nasty past. And nothing is greater than the opportunities for growth and ecstasy that await us when we are willing to be aware of everything just as it is.

8

CHANNELING

When you read someone's palms, you reflect his character and life story with clarity and compassion. You add nothing but perspective. It is the absence of comment from your personal peanut gallery that makes a psychic reading different from an ordinary rehash of your friend's life, and it is also what makes your psychic readings accurate. Since you are passing along pre-existent information rather than making it up, you are functioning as a *channel*. A channel is a passageway. Many types of material can be transported through a channel without affecting the channel itself; a channel does not alter the material it transports. The more open a channel is, the more goods can be carried through it. Conversely, if a channel is stormy or clogged with debris, smooth transportation is impossible.

The lines channel energy on the hands, and you channel energy in your life. When you are an open channel, tremendous energy flows through you. When, however, you use yourself as a garbage dump or when flurries of emotion ruffle your waters, your energy is blocked or wasted, and you don't feel right. You need the Cosmic Harbor Patrol to dredge your waters. You might doubt that you are a channel of cosmic energy, but look at the evidence. You are alive. You're awake and alert enough to read this book. Not only that, you've already made it to Chapter 8. What more could you ask for? But don't get too excited about yourself right away—rocks channel cosmic energy, too. It's all a question of degree.

In your personal life, you are free to use your cosmic energy any way you wish. You can laugh, cry, eat pizza, make money, make love or go surfing. Everything you do is your way of channeling the energy at the moment you do it, and how you channel it is generally your own business. During a psychic reading, however, you bring someone else into the picture by offering to channel for him. This significantly increases your responsibility to channel clearly. It's true that other people are always dogpaddling through our channels by being involved in our lives, but this is different. In ordinary relationships it is clear to all parties that anything you say is your personal opinion, and is not necessarily true. At least it should be clear.

During a psychic palmreading this situation is altered. If someone wanted your opinion about his life, he'd ask for it. Notice that he didn't. If he lets you read his hands, he's looking for *truth.* Now truth is a touchy subject in any case, so at the start you'd better disabuse your friend of the idea that there's an absolute truth about his personality. On the mundane plane, all that's true is that he was born and he's going to die, and on the absolute plane, what's true is that he is beginningless, will never die, and that his essential nature is Divine Love. But it is what's between the rock and the absolute that probably interests him most. Forget birth and death, he wants to know about that red Ferrari. Work with him from where he is—he'll get to birth and death anyway.

You are a *channel*, not a broadcaster, so keep your personal opinions out of the reading. Sense the other person's situation with compassion and detachment so that you can see how *he* thinks his problems arose, without falling into his storyline yourself. People listen much more closely when you hold their hands as you talk. When you study their hands as a palmist, they listen even harder. Even if you've never read a palm before, if you pore over the lines you'll be seen as a fortuneteller, and even if the individual thinks fortunetelling is bunk, he'll be listening more closely than usual—just in case. Many people are so unaccustomed to looking at the truth within themselves that they think it's somewhere outside. When you read their palms they may peg you as a potential source. Whatever you say comes from them, but they rarely notice this. Part of your role as a channeler is to support people in seeing that they already contain all the truth they require.

When you are channeling for a person, you are at his service. Whether you read palms at a party or in private, take your responsibility seriously. The person you're reading for already knows everything you are going to tell him, but he probably does not know that he knows it. Your job is to remind him of what he's ready to be reminded of so that he can see his life from a positive perspective. This might enable him to make choices or to accept his circumstances more easily. (Maybe that ten million dollar inheritance wasn't so bad, after all.) He will remember what you say long after you've forgotten it, so be kind, be careful, and keep your opinions out of the reading. Behave with love and you will be remembered with love. In the following pages you will find a few exercises that will help you channel more clearly.

Swimming the Psychic Channel: Warmups

The channeling you do during a reading is of a special kind, and it requires some special preparation. The preparation includes both specific exercises and guidelines for personal comportment during the reading. We'll cover two major preparatory exercises: Grounding in the Three Centers and Painting the White Light. In addition, we'll discuss important points about attitude, speech, and the ethics of palmreading, before we move on to a step-by-step description of how to do a psychic palmreading.

The precaution that precedes all precautions is this: *Do not read for someone who does not want to be read.* If a person is clearly aware that he does not want a reading, he will create mental resistance which will prevent you from reading him accurately anyway. Then his negative expectations about the reading will be fulfilled and both of you will have an unpleasant experience. Who needs it? If he doesn't want a reading, don't read him. Even more important is the fact that neither you nor anyone else has the right to probe another person's character without his cooperation and consent. Psychic pushiness does not pay.

Respect resistance within yourself as well. If you are certain that you don't want to do the reading, don't do it. Pushing against your instinctive knowledge rarely brings positive results. So before the reading, be sure that both of you have the opportunity to speak then or forever hold your peace. Once you've both acknowledged that you want the reading to happen, begin the preparatory exercises.

Grounding in the Three Centers

Suppose you're going to give someone a piggyback ride. You're not sure how much the person weighs, you don't know whether he's going to flail around once you get him on your back, you don't know if he's going to hold on and make your job easier or lean back and do gymnastics while you try to hold him up. It's a chancy proposition at best, but what the heck, you decide to play. What do you do first?

You might ask your passenger to cooperate with you and explain that it will help if he doesn't kick you in the spine while you're galloping. He'll understand, yet people are capricious; he might forget and bolt. Your best protection is to be prepared for anything. Bend your knees, drop your weight, and center yourself. Then you can sway with him from side to side, and you're much less likely to fall. Without realizing it, you always center yourself before you lift something heavy, because you know instinctively that if you try to carry a weighty load without balancing yourself first, you will fall.

Pause for a moment and imagine that you're about to lift a sack of concrete, or a large child, or a not-so-portable typewriter. How does your posture change? You drop your weight and brace your lower body to accommodate the load. Settling the weight and centering the energy are also prerequisites to doing a psychic palmreading. You do not know in advance what will happen during the reading—the guy could be the Incredible Hulk in the middle of a hypoglycemia attack, and as long as the reading lasts you are channeling for both you and him.

If you center yourself before beginning the reading, you can read for nearly anyone without losing either your energy or your cool. Whatever the person is going through is fine; it is his manifestation of Divine Consciousness at that moment. Even if it looks bleak, he'll pull through eventually. As the Chinese sage, Lao

Tzu, said, "No rainstorm lasts forever." Even in Seattle. However, just because your friend is acting out Hurricane Betsy (or John) doesn't mean you have to get soaked, too. The following exercises are psychic storm windows.

Grounding in the Navel Center

We begin the exercise by warming up the navel center. This is not a bunch of buildings in Annapolis, but is an essential part of your body. Located about three inches below the navel, it is the focus of our grounding, strength and protection. Just as a tree needs roots to keep from being downed by the first pack of marauding squirrels, we need firm grounding in our center to keep us balanced. To be steadily aware of one's center is to be grounded.

Unless it is grounded, an electrical wire is both dangerous and useless. The least it can do is fly around shaking off sparks, and the most it can do is electrocute someone. A person without grounding is not quite as dangerous as the stray hot wire (particularly if you wear rubber gloves when you handle him), but he's not very helpful either. Ungrounded people are likely to be indecisive, insecure, and airy-fairy. Ninety-second TV commercials tax their concentration. Small gusts of wind knock them down. Although grounding is always advantageous, it is essential when doing psychic readings, because unless we are firmly centered, we can be thrown off balance by the influx of another person's energy.

There are a lot of ungrounded people walking the pavement right now. They're not ungrounded because grounding is hard to find; they're ungrounded because they haven't looked for it. Or if they have, they've been looking for it in car dealerships, movie theaters, and bars instead of (how boring) within themselves. It's so much fun to look everywhere else, but unfortunately looking outside never works. The only place to find stability and balance is within ourselves, because that's where it begins.

Recall a moment when you were about to trip but you got your balance; feel that sense of steadiness again. Now remember a time when you felt perfectly tranquil (okay, relatively tranquil); feel that moment of tranquility again. Put your attention in your navel center, about three inches below your navel and two inches inside. Even if you're not sure whether you feel anything there but indigestion, focus your mind there. Imagine this area as a red-orange sun, glowing powerfully with a steady light. Feel the area become warmer. Let your attention rest in this area until you feel your body weight sinking slightly. The more you practice focusing on this area, the easier it will be.

You can center yourself at any time simply by remembering your center. As you dash for the green light or reach for the cookie jar or begin to bristle at a co-worker or friend, stop and *center*. Take a deep breath, imagine the red-gold sun and feel your center glow bright. This is truly the pause that refreshes, and it will prepare you to ground yourself more thoroughly before psychic readings.

Hearing the Heart

After you have grounded in the navel center, draw your attention to the heart. The heart center is in the center of the chest. It is the gathering point for the energy of love and compassion. When it is activated, we feel light, happy, generous and compassionate. We laugh a lot from sheer joy. Other people feel great when they're around us. When the heart center is contracted or drained, we feel sad, sorry, angry and unwilling to love. Other people notice this and often decide to read a good book instead of spending time with us. We can activate our hearts at any time by deciding to be open to love.

The most effective way to keep the heart center activated is to love. Love, love, love. When people yell at you, love them. When they disappoint you, love them. When you hate yourself, love yourself. When love seems like the stupidest, most dangerous course to take, love. This does not mean acting like an infatuated fool. It means maintaining an open, compassionate attitude toward all that happens and it indicates a willingness to take things as they are.

Put your attention in your heart center. Now imagine a time when you felt a sudden surge of affection. Feel the love in your heart. Think of someone you love. As you do this, feel your heart become warm. Imagine it glowing with a yellow-gold light. See this light illuminate your body and become a halo around you. This is the light of love. Feel it gathering in your heart.

An open heart is essential to an accurate psychic reading because during the reading you become aware of the other person's frailties. If you read well, his fears, doubts, disappointments, blocks and upsets will appear to you along with his talents and joy. Put yourself in his position. If someone glanced at your hands at a party, or even in a private session, you wouldn't want him to glibly reel off your ten deepest fears. Keep your attention in the golden glow of your heart and the appropriate kindness and warmth will arise.

The Third Eye

The third eye center is located on the forehead between your other two eyes. Your other eyes cannot see it, but it can see them. It doesn't need contact lenses—only your attention and willingness to see. The third eye is the gathering point for the energy of intuition and insight. When it is fully activated, telepathy, precognition, aura analysis and other whizbang psychic skills are a cinch. The more activated your third eye center is, the more psychic you are. As you cultivate your psychic skills, you will be able to feel the third eye as a little nugget of tissue inside your forehead. It is associated with the pineal gland, which physicians claim is left over from when we were fish, and which yogis claim is the source of extrasensory powers. All we need is to find a fish that bends spoons and they can both be right.

The Blank Screen Exercise

This is a powerful exercise for enhancing your awareness of the third eye. Put your attention in the third eye point between your eyebrows. Imagine it as an open space. Now imagine a blank movie screen in that space. Imagine the screen turning red. Then erase it. Now make it orange. Erase it. Then turn it green, then yellow, blue, and then finally color it a rich purplish-blue. Watch the purple-blue light for a moment and then erase the screen again. Now picture the face of someone you know well being projected on the screen. What is he doing? After you've watched for a moment, erase the screen again.

During a palmreading, while you are holding the hands, keep part of your attention focused on the screen in your third eye. You might begin to see images, dates, numbers, words, maybe even Tahitian vacation spots moving across the screen. If you or the person you're reading for has a particular question, ask it internally and look at the screen. You might find an answer written there or you may hear a voice telling you an answer. Beware, however, of voices from the monkey mind masquerading as couriers for the inner self. If you hear, "Wouldn't you really rather drive a Buick?", erase the screen and start again, unless the question in mind was, "Should I buy a Datsun?" As you practice this exercise you will develop a clearer sense of which answers come truly from your intuitive self and which come from the chattering mind.

For most of us, the energy centers are constantly in flux, neither fully opened nor fully closed. As we expand our awareness, they become more open, more of the time. You needn't demand complete openness from yourself all at once. Love where you are, and you'll automatically open up at exactly the pace you can handle. There are seven major energy centers in the body; we have discussed the three that pertain most directly to doing psychic readings.*

Review of the Grounding Exercise

Put your attention in your navel center. Feel the strength, protection and balance that the red-orange glow there brings. Feel yourself centered and linked to the earth. Pause for a moment and feel the warmth in your navel center. Then imagine the navel center closing slightly and sending energy up into your heart.

Feel the energy move into your heart, filling it with the golden glow of compassion and life. Feel your heart as a golden flower open in the sun, and then feel it expand to become the sun. Feel the warmth and the strength of its glow.

Next, let the energy rise to the third eye, warming and activating your intuition in a blue-purple light. Feel it as a tiny glow-

*For more information on energy and its passage through the seven centers, see *Kundalini: The Secret of Life* by Swami Muktananda and *Energy Ecstasy and Your Seven Vital Centers* by Bernard Gunther. Both available through Book People, 2940 7th Street, Berkeley, California 94710.

ing meteorite between your eyes, just inside your skull. Then let the meteorite be transformed into a blank white movie screen, receptive to the energy at hand. Pause and feel the clarity of your third eye.

During a palmreading, you will circulate the energy through your body once more just before you begin to speak, grounding and stabilizing first in the navel center, then opening into the heart and finally becoming the clear screen in the third eye. Psychic readings should come from the heart and the third eye, not from the navel center. Notice that the mouth, through which we speak, is located between the heart and the third eye. Thus, our words should be born from the marriage of compassion and insight.

Negativity: Return to Sender

After you've stabilized your energy in the three centers, one more preliminary exercise remains. You will create a protective energy field around your body by visualizing a mantle of white light. The white light symbolizes the protective power of love, and visualizing it is an ancient technique for sealing the aura against potentially disruptive forces. Most people don't mean to be disruptive, and indeed would think you were nuts if you accused them of disfiguring your aura, but disfigure it they can—if you let them. The aura is a living, shifting field of energy and it can be affected by its surroundings. Unless you create a strong energy field around yourself, you can lose energy by osmosis during a reading.

If you pour a pitcher of cold water into a pot of hot water, the hot water will get colder and the cold will get hotter. Similarly, if one person is burning with distress and he contacts someone who's cool and calm, the disturbed person is likely to calm down, but the calmer person risks absorbing some ''heat'' from his upset brother and getting upset himself. This need not happen, and it will not happen if the calmer person is securely grounded in his own center and is shielded from the onslaught of the other's upset. If you play your cards right, you can calm another person without upsetting yourself. The white light exercise will help you.

Imagine the halo which surrounds the steady flame of a candle. See how the light shines smooth and gold, rising from the heart of the flame. Now imagine the light of the bright sun at noon. Feel the fearless sunlight illuminating everything around it. Now imagine that your body is a candle wick that can never burn up. Feel your body lit up by the power of the sun. See the halo of brilliant light emanating from your body and forming a steady halo around your every cell. Your body is like the burning bush that can never be consumed. See this halo extend as far as you can imagine, and know that this light is the light of love. Wear the white light as a royal mantle of clarity, protection and force.

The white light exercise works like magic. As soon as you visualize the light, it's there. The strength of your visualization determines the strength of the light, so imagine brightly. Cover every bit of yourself, leave no Achilles' heel. Do not begin the palmreading until you can see the white light around you. You need cover only yourself to do a psychic reading, but the white light can be painted over anything and anyone whom you wish to protect. Imagine it around children, friends, dogs, cats, fish, airplanes, bowling balls, anything you care about. If you ever find that you cannot complete the halo around an object, there may already be a defect in it. If you cannot complete the light around a person, he may be ill or in danger. Pour in extra blessings until you see the light expand.

Sometimes, despite all our precautions, a stray dart flies through. A person tells his life story and suddenly we want to cry, or sleep the rest of the day, even though we did our grounding and our white light exercises like the good little psychics we are. If you have taken your precautions, the only upsets that can still pierce your shield are the ones you have not dealt with in yourself. If your mother died and you haven't handled your own grief and anger, you will be upset when you do a reading for someone else whose mother died. If you keep choosing lovers who reject you and you have not admitted that to yourself and seen the pattern, then you might have a violent response to the complaints of someone else who does the same thing. You'll probably think he's a real fool.

If someone's story upsets you and you cannot shake it off, examine your own life. What are the similarities between his life and yours? The instant you acknowledge your fellowship with him and see the truth about yourself, your distress will pass. "Upsetting" people often come to us as gifts, since watching our response to them encourages our own growth.

Palmistry Etiquette Guide

In addition to preparing yourself for the reading through energy exercises, consider how you will behave toward your friend. People always respond to choice of words, tone of voice and gestures, but they are even more sensitive to nuance during a psychic reading. To ensure that you convey your meaning with as much clarity and kindness as possible, consider these topics:

Tempo. Don't rush. Look at the hands and feel the energy carefully before you speak. Once you say something, you can't really take it back, so make sure that what you say is what you mean and that what you mean is what the palms mean. If you don't have time to read someone carefully, don't read him at all.

Person's Background. Assess the person's age, probable educational background and emotional state, and adjust your tone and vocabulary accordingly. Your reading will help you here. People with sharply curving head lines will find blunt statements hard to swallow and will probably exaggerate the gravity of what you say. Understate. Those with firm square hands and straightforward lines will be impatient if you don't get right to the point. If you have any bad news, such as probable illness or an approaching island or bar in a major line, preface it with a statement about the person's capacity to change his life and with something good about the hands, such as a good basic shape or a strong thumb. You can find something positive to say about everyone. Many people overlook the fact that good and bad usually come together, and that good often comes ultimately from experiences which seem painful or unnecessary when they happen.

Tone of Voice. In addition to your words, consider your tone of voice; it reflects the quality of your breathing. If your breath is deep and slow, then your voice is rich and low. It will have a comforting ring to the person you're reading for. Be aware of changes in your voice; if you start to speak rapidly you make it hard for the person to understand you. If your voice takes on a higher pitch, you're getting nervous. Slow down. You'll never get a clear beam on your intuition if words are tumbling from your mind and mouth in high-pitched shallow gasps. Initially, your tone of voice will have more emotional impact on the person than the meaning of the words you say, so don't squeak.

Touch. You also influence your friend by your touch. Ideally your hands will be warm, flexible and calming to him. Realistically speaking, however, there are times when we all get cold, clammy and nervous. If you can't steady your breath and warm your hands, try to avoid doing the reading. If you can't avoid the reading, at least keep your hands off your friend.

Feedback. Be open to receiving feedback. If you suspect that the person doesn't understand what you mean, ask him to repeat your statement back to you in his own words. Keep talking back and forth until you agree that what he understands is what you mean. When you channel for someone, what matters is *his* understanding of what you say and the positive use to which the reading can be put in his everyday life.

Possible Error. Everybody makes mistakes, even you and I. Sometimes you might not be paying attention, or you might speak without thinking, or you might misinterpret something that you looked at carefully. You will learn more, faster, if you admit that you might be wrong. If someone says that he doesn't agree with something you've read, just say, ''Perhaps I was mistaken . . .'' and move on. It may be that you're right but the person isn't ready to hear what you're saying. It is his privilege not to accept what you say about him. Whatever the reason for the ''error,'' you'll only get yourself in deeper by trying to justify it.

Foretelling Death. Never predict the date of death. Even if you think you know when someone will die, keep the news to yourself. You might be wrong and the hands might change. Most of all, no one has the right to create fear, or possibly a self-fulfilling prophecy, in someone else by guessing the time of death aloud. Doing so is irresponsible and inexcusable. Just assure the curious that someday they will die, and suggest that they enjoy the time before them.

Respect. Respect everyone equally. No matter how simple, boring or rude a person may seem to you, he's the only him he's got. The Divine Consciousness breathing through him is the same as that which breathes through you, so by respecting him you respect yourself. Address yourself to the Divinity within him and you bring that Divinity out.

Changeability. Like everything else, the hands can change. Be sure that the person you're reading for knows this as clearly as you do.

Keep these points in mind as you go on with the reading, as all of them contribute to your attitude and bearing. If you want the person to truly listen and understand what you say, then create an atmosphere of clarity, respect and love.

On With the Show

After you have completed the grounding exercise and painted your white light (these take less time to do than to read about), and you have mentally reviewed the Palmistry Etiquette Guide, you are ready to begin the reading. What follows is a step-by-step summary of what to do both internally and externally when reading someone's palms. It's best to read this section several times until you are familiar with it—I do not recommend that you prop the book up next to you while you do the palmreading. That's like trying to follow the instructions in a sex manual while clutching the book tightly in hand. Get comfortable with the basic pattern of the reading and you will gradually make it your own. Mastery comes with practice. The best way to master palmreading is to read a lot of palms. So read the book, set it aside, and look over all those lovely hands. Return to the book for reminders whenever you like, but the best way to learn about the hands is by looking at them.

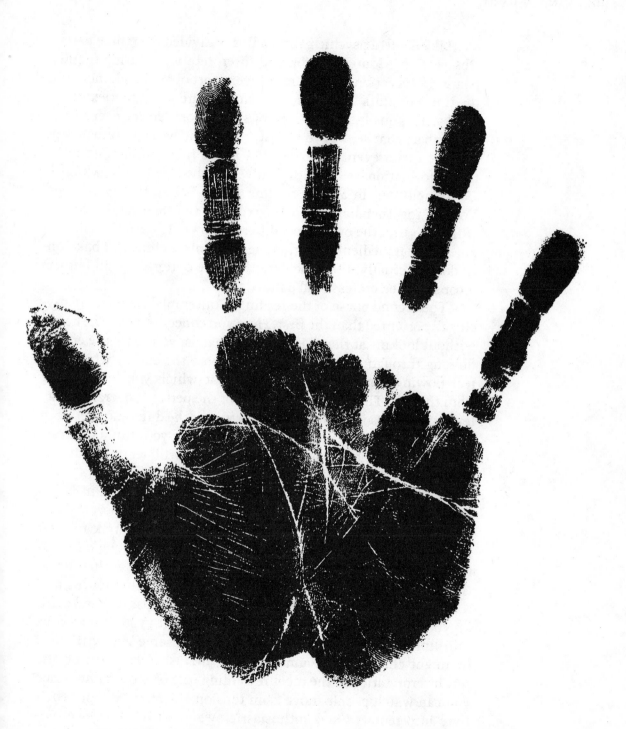

Notice the spatulate hand shape, the strong early life line, and the head line curving toward Luna in the compact hand of television personality Regis Philbin.

Like Gaul, a psychic palmreading is divided into three parts—Observation, Contemplation and Interpretation. During the first phase, Observation, you examine every part of the hand, including the lines, mounts, marks, color, temperature, texture, flexibility, hand shape, quadrants and type of skin lotion. Notice everything, remember what strikes you most, notice the basic patterns of the life, the major events, all the news that's fit to observe, then set this information aside until you've finished part two, which is Contemplation. In a way, reading palms is like baking cookies. You put together some of the ingredients and then set them aside while you mix the others in a different bowl. Then at the end you put all the ingredients together, add chocolate chips and bake until done. Actually, the chocolate chips are optional for all but the most seasoned professional palmists.

The second phase of the reading, Contemplation, is more psychically oriented than the first. Here you concentrate on the hands without looking at them. Holding the hands, you sense the energy flowing through them. Then you compare the energy which you feel flowing from the right side to that which you feel flowing from the left. This gives you a sense of the person's overall energy level as well as giving you a clear picture of the difference between his internal and external polarities. The stiller your mind is during the Contemplation phase, the more you will learn about the person.

The third part of the reading is Interpretation. Until this point, you have been primarily concerned with observing and sensing the hands. In the third phase you begin to talk to your friend. The purpose of the Interpretation is to pass along information about your friend's character and about trends in his life so that he understands you and can use the information for his personal benefit and growth. By speaking with compassion and clarity, you share your perceptions appropriately with your friend, thus fulfilling your role as a channel. If you don't serve him with love, he might change the channel. In fact, he just might turn off the set. Interpretation is the most rewarding part of the reading, since you can watch people move from tension and anxiety about their lives into renewed and enthusiastic awareness of their own natural magnificence. Goethe once said that if you respond to someone as he presents himself to you, he will stay as he is or sink

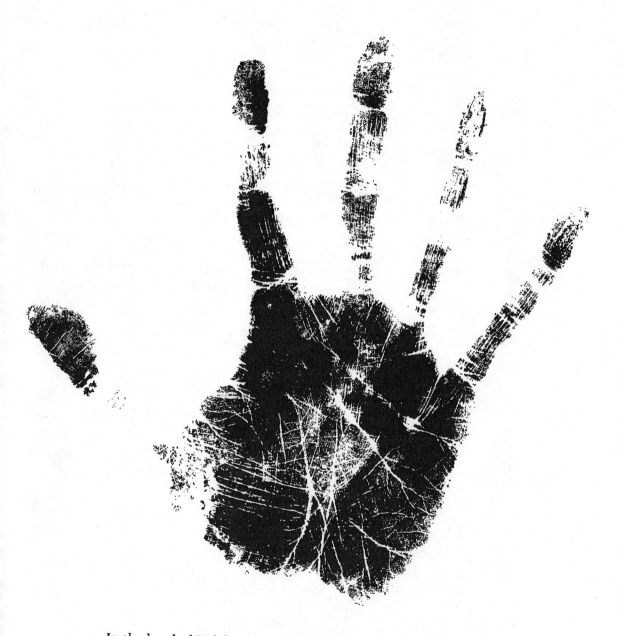

In the hand of Vidal Sassoon, entrepreneur and hair designer, we see long fingers and fine lines, showing sensitivity and an eye for detail. His career skyrocketed around age 35; notice how the life and fate lines become stronger at that point.

lower, but if you address yourself to what you know is the best in him, he will rise to his highest capacity. Speak to God within the person and you bring God out.

Hand in Hand: Step by Step

Phase One: Observation

In which you look at everything your friend imagined could appear on his hands, and more.

Within Yourself:
Let your mind become still.

Take several deep breaths.

Remember your unity with your friend. Even if he beat you at tennis last week, he's still your brother.

Keep half your attention circulating between your heart and your third eye and half of it focused out toward the hands.

Scan the hands. Note the relative strength of the quadrants, the temperature, sweatiness, skin texture, length of fingers and posture of the fingers. Compare the two hands.

To Your Friend:
Smile, then explain briefly that the lines and mounts can change, so he has control over his own life.

Ask if he is right- or left-handed and how old he is. This tells you which side is dominant and approximately where he is on his lifeline.

Lapse into a companionable silence. Let your friend know by the quality of your silence that you are with him and are interested in his life.

Cradle his hands in your own as though his hands were little children.

Identify the basic hand type: Square, spatulate, conic, or pointed.

Identify the shape of the fingertips.

Look at the set of the fingers, noticing which fingers lean toward each other, which, if any, stick out from the hand, and which are playing one finger keep moving.

If your friend gets restless, tell him you always look carefully before you talk, so silence doesn't mean bad news.

Bend each finger slowly, listening with your inner sense for the degree of flexibility or tension. Remember which fingers are exceptionally rigid or floppy on each hand.

Look at, perhaps run your fingers over, every mount, noting the fullness or firmness of each one:
Venus
Luna
Upper Mars
Lower Mars

You still haven't said a word about the hands. Or about the weather.

Check all the mounts under the fingers. Note any peculiar marks on the mounts, such as stars, crosses, grids, or test patterns.

You're waiting until you get the whole picture before talking.

Look at the lines.

Note their clarity, depth, and where they begin and end.

Look for breaks, branches, dots, bars, islands and so forth. Notice any color changes in the lines such as dark, red or puffy white areas.

Examine the:
Life line
Heart line
Head line
Fate line
Inner life line
Line of Apollo
Health line
Marriage lines
Children lines

Also look for lines of influence, noticing where they begin and end. If there are many extra lines, don't try to read each one; remember that a network of lines shows a highstrung personality.

Maintain a calm silence.

Hold his hands warmly and he can sit there forever.

Look for the special marks:
Girdle of Venus
Ring of Solomon
Mystic Triangle
Healers' Marks
Marks of Inheritance.

After you've looked at and listened to everything, take a deep breath and let the information come together in your mind. Go back to the things that particularly caught your attention (tense or flaccid fingers, broken lines, unusual marks and so forth).

You might see evidence of an important event or theme while observing the hands. These could include breaks in the life line, a heart line ending under Saturn, a very stiff nondominant thumb, and others. The contemplation phase of the reading will give you more insight into the origin of these patterns.

Mentally set this information aside, allowing it to arrange itself while you move on to the next phase of the reading.

Keep holding the hands with warmth and love.

Phase Two: Contemplation

In which you close your eyes and feel the energy flowing from your friend's hands.

Within Yourself:
Close your eyes. Relax.

To Your Friend:
Hold the hands lightly, with your thumbs over the center of your friend's palms.

Repeat the grounding exercise briefly: send energy to the navel, then the heart, then the third eye.

Breathe deeply.

Ask internally, "How can I serve this person today?"
This question orients you toward the true purpose of the reading, which is to reflect back just what is appropriate for the person at that time.

Continue to hold the hands gently.

If you don't hear an answer the first time you ask, relax, breathe deeply, look at the screen in your third eye and ask again. If you still don't hear anything, don't worry. Keep asking the question at every reading and someday you'll hear a valid response.

After asking how you can serve, move on to the Energy Circulation Exercise. This is a variation of the Energy Circulation Exercise in the last chapter, so it will be easy for you.

This exercise is designed to create an energy circuit between you and your friend which will enable you to sense the strength and the frequency of the energy traveling through his hands. This energy reflects the energy balance of his entire body.

During the exercise, stay open to whatever feelings, words or images come to you. There is no right or wrong result; every experience is unique.

Energy Circulation Exercise

Keep your feet flat on the floor.

Hold your friend's hands, placing your thumbtips in the middle of his palms.

Take a deep breath. Relax.

Put your attention in your own hands. Feel them become warm.

After your own hands have warmed up and you feel open and relaxed, put your attention on your friend.

In most of the previous exercises, you have formed an energy circuit within your own body, moving energy from navel to heart to third eye. Your major focus will continue to be within your own body, but you are now ready to include in the circuit one more person.

Put your attention in your hands, particularly in your thumbs as they rest on the hands of your friends.

Imagine that they are powerful antennae, sensing the energy of your friend's hand.

Look at the blank screen in your third eye as you continue to sense the energy of the hands.

You might receive impressions about the person's

Your hands may move spontaneously during the exercise to feel various parts of the hands; let them.

Feel where your hands touch his: know that he is there.

mood, or get a sense of energy pulsating at a particular rate, or perceive colors and sounds. You might even pick up a message from departed Aunt Agnes. (Something like, "My dear, the laundry ticket is in my blue coat.")

Whatever you feel or see, it is produced by the unique intersection of your energy and your friend's. So enjoy it—it won't happen again. (In certain cases that's an advantage.)

Right and Left

It's oscillation time. Move your attention from the right hand to the left. Feel any differences in the energy flow. For most people, energy from the right side represents the personality they present to the world, and energy from the left represents the inner life.

This exercise may add insight to the observation phase of the reading. For example, suppose you observe that the thumb of the nondominant hand is rigid and held down. This tells you the person is suppressing his inner will, but not *why*.

Here is a case history showing how the energy circulation exercise could clarify your perceptions of a person whose hand you are studying. Suppose that you are reading for a young woman, and that during the energy circulation exercise you see an image of a domineering man, or glimpse a scene in which a small child is threatened. You might also feel a rapid pulsation of energy coming from the nondominant side while the pulsations on the dominant side are slow and lethargic. (Anything can come up during the exercise; this is an example from my own experience.)

The vision of the domineering man tells you that your friend is still under the repressive influence of some father figure. This could be an actual father, a stepfather, an employer, or a husband. The more conscious she becomes of inhibiting her natural exuberance in the effort to please this patiarchal figure, the less suppressed she will feel.

Variations between the pulsation rates of the energy tell you more about how her will is repressed. It pulses on the internal side like the heart of an excited bird, but it manifests itself on the outside like the munching of a bored cow. The frequency on the nondominant side reveals what the person is really feeling. In this case, she is feeling excited and has excess energy internally; this energy is blocked somewhere between its origin in her true self and its manifestation in the self she presents.

Reminding her of her inner vitality can be quite helpful. Suggest that she really look within herself and see what she wants to do. Recommend that she dance around her living room every day.

Remember, however, that you are not a psychotherapist (unless you are, in which case be sure to remember that), so don't give too much advice. As much as possible, let your fingers do the walking and your true self do the talking.

After you've received all the information you feel is available, or after a long time has gone by and nothing has happened, open your eyes, sit up straight, hold the hands loosely and move on to phase three: Interpretation. Even if you think nothing happened during this exercise other than a catnap, you might be surprised to find out how much you know when you start talking to your friend.

Phase Three: Interpretation

In which you translate the information you've received while observing and contemplating the hands, and interpret it for your friend in such a way that he or she can use it for greater personal expansion.

Within Yourself:

Gather in your mind the information you received from both observing and contemplating the hands.

Remember any patterns or recurring themes. Relationships among all the factors may become clearer as you talk.

When you have a general idea of what you're going to say, size the person up and decide what's the best way to express yourself. Be kind.

Continue to keep half your attention focused on your heart and third eye and half focused out toward your friend.

Let your intuition guide you about where to begin. Every hand is unique, every reading takes place at a unique intersection of time, space and mind. There's no set pattern

To Your Friend:

Hang in there (to the hand).

Tell him what the palm told you, speaking slowly and clearly, and asking him if he understands you every time he gives you a blank stare. You should even check with him if he nods all the time. It could be a tic.

to follow when letting the palm's message through, so follow your intuition.

You can begin with the life line, describing general vitality and life history, and then proceed to the mental, emotional, vocational and marital history. If a particular issue pops to mind, begin there.

Continue to breathe deeply and speak in a warm tone of voice.

Don't ramble.

Ask yourself:
Is what I am saying appropriate to his life at this time?

Am I serving him by telling him this?

Listen for the answers in your heart and your third eye. If you receive specific guidance for your friend, say, "Thank you," to whatever source it came from and tactfully pass the guidance along. This is a basic courtesy. If you ask for a gift and receive it, then acknowledge it and use it.

As you speak, look up from the hands occasionally and glance at your friend. Make sure he's still with you. Make sure you're still with him.

Be sure that:
What you say is what you mean.

What you mean is what the marks and the energy of the palms mean.

You have opened to your inner self and are channeling clearly and accurately.

When you've said everything you have to say . . .

Ask your friend if he has any further questions.

If the question can be answered directly from the palm, then answer it. Many people wonder how many marriage lines they have, or whether they're likely to have a job change soon. These are easily answered by examining the lines.

As long as you make it clear that the hands show probabilities, not certainties, and that people often change their lines by transforming their lives, these are harmless questions to answer. However, if you do not know the answer, don't fake it. Say so.

If someone asks about death or seems to be asking you to take responsibility for a major decision, or even seems to be grasping for a life preserver from you, refer him back to his own inner self. It is his best medicine and his best friend.

Suggest that he meditate quietly on his own center and let guidance arise from within. Meditation, exercise and careful diet will support him in receiving this guidance; let him know this. If he asks internally for guidance or a sign, he will eventually receive it.

When you feel you've reached a natural completion of the reading, tell your friend you feel that's all for now. Ask if he feels that the reading is complete. If not, briefly clear up the loose ends; usually they were discussed earlier and he's forgotten about it.

When he feels complete too, give him back his hands. You couldn't coordinate four, anyway. Smile and stand up.

You might want to hug each other now, hands and all.

Your friend already knows everything you're going to tell him, if not consciously, then through his inner self. If he didn't know it at some level, he wouldn't recognize it as true when you tell it to him. So you're not telling him anything he doesn't already know, you're just reminding him. The more confident you are of these facts, the more enjoyable your readings will be, and the less tempted you'll be to add your personal interpretation to the facts at hand. Some commentary is necessary in every reading, but keep it to a minimum.

The more able you are to see people exactly as they are, the more clearly you will see the essential beauty within them. As you see more beauty in them, you will be able to love them more. And the more love you give to all, the clearer your insight will be and the more love you will receive. Reading the hands is one way to see people very clearly and to use this vision as a vehicle for experiencing greater love for all humanity. So read a lot of palms, emanate a lot of love, and your channel will be tops in the ratings. You might even make prime-time.

9

MEDITATION

You have already done a form of meditation by contemplating the hands. This meditation, however, was focused outside yourself. The next step in expanding your awareness is to focus inwardly and rediscover the source of happiness within yourself.

Of all the practices that deepen awareness of oneself and the world, meditation is the most effective. Meditation is the realization of one's true self. The deeper our meditation, the more aware we become of our connection to all beings and things. The clearer that awareness becomes, the happier, stabler, more productive and more energetic we become. During meditation the transitory and misleading parts of our personalities come to the surface and drift away, laying bare our original nature, which is blissful and calm. Transitory and misleading thoughts include thinking that we should never have been born, that we are alone and unloved in the universe, and believing that the life we are living is not the one we signed up for, and that our real life was obviously given to someone else. Such thoughts do nothing but cloud the mind. They do not get us on the cover of *Vogue*. Through meditation, we tune in to the inner cosmic rhythm; then we can keep a steady beat no matter what the rest of the band is playing.

Although spontaneous meditation can happen in many situations, including driving, watching the sea, or doing any concentrated work, there are distinct advantages to setting aside a part of every day with the specific intention of practicing meditation. Daily meditation creates the space in which many conflicts in our lives can sort themselves out without our conscious effort. By meditating every day we give ourselves respite from active thought and show a willingness to receive wisdom from our inner selves.

During the past nine years I have meditated regularly. Through meditation, many cobwebs and fears have lifted from my heart. Those that remain are now more available for observation. Knowing that my fears and insecurities are not my true self makes it easier to examine them with interest rather than anxiety. I also attribute much of my accuracy as a psychic palmist to the regular practice of meditation. There is no formal link between meditation and palmistry, but certain skills that are enhanced through meditation are also useful when reading palms. The ability to focus the mind completely on one object without being carried away by personal thoughts is one of the most wonderful by-products of meditation. Related to this is the ability to tune out distracting sights and sounds. Moreover, extended practice of meditation makes it easier to switch modes within one's mind, that is, to go from analytical, rational thought to intuitive awareness. All of these skills are indispensable to an accurate and insightful palmreader. Clearly, they are useful in every other area of life as well.

The benefits of meditation are both powerful and subtle, and they begin as soon as you begin your practice. (They may be more subtle than powerful at first, but keep up and you'll see a difference.) If you want to be a good psychic palmist, meditate. If you want to sleep half as much and have twice the energy, meditate. If you want to go beyond the Pause Button and the Troubles Game and experience the ecstasy beyond expansion and contraction, meditate. Many daily routines are healthy and beneficial, but none equals the value of daily meditation. In a world full of false cures, it really is good for what ails you. This is because it returns you to the awareness of the Divine within yourself.

To Meditate or Not to Meditate

Many of us have reasons why we don't meditate, and some of them sound plausible. We say we don't have the time, we can't sit in full lotus posture, it's against our religion, we're allergic to it, we'd get bored, and so forth. What most of these reasons boil down to is fear. Once a person begins to meditate and passes through the early period of her practice, her reservations about meditation melt in the face of the bounteous rewards she receives.

As for meditation taking too much time, if you meditate thirty minutes daily, your sleep needs will eventually decrease by two or more hours per night. Your mental clarity will increase, so your waking time will be twice as productive. That adds up to a net savings of many happy and productive hours in return for a paltry half hour of meditation. Just think of the benefits if you sat for an hour.

As for posture, there is no need to sit in the lotus posture or any other posture that causes you unremitting discomfort. Any posture in which you can sit comfortably with a straight spine for an extended period of time is fine. That means you can meditate sitting in a straight-backed chair, sitting cross-legged on the floor, or even lying flat on your back. Just keep your spine straight and you can do what you like. Just because Indian statues sit in full lotus posture doesn't mean you have to.

Since meditation is not a religion, there is no possible conflict between meditation and practicing your religion. If you don't believe in God, then meditation will give you greater confidence and inner calm. If you do believe in God, meditation will enhance your experience of Divine Love so that you feel more in communion with God, whatever you conceive Her to be. Meditation is not a dogma or a ritual—it is the rediscovery of your True Self.

As in other unfamiliar activities, the biggest barrier to exploring meditation is fear. Unstated or unacknowledged fears are the most damaging of all. These might include the fear of finding something awful if we look inside ourselves ("Who knows, I could be the Elephant Man in disguise"), fear of change, fear of having bizarre experiences, and fear of being considered a weirdo for meditating. Greater than all these fears, however, is the fear of fear. For most of us, the fear of being afraid far exceeds any of our actual fears. This fear is powerful because it has no clear object, and because we resist experiencing it due to a belief that it is bad to be afraid. Some of us are also afraid that if we began to experience our fears just a little, we'd be inundated by them and never be heard from again. The fact is that fear is finite, and that once we observe and feel it, it's the fear that disappears, not us. Remember that fear is contraction, so fear of fear adds contraction to contraction and makes us shrivel up. Mark Twain once said that courage is not the absence of fear, it is the mastery of fear. We might add that courage is also the willingness to observe fear within ourselves.

Fear of fear is more destructive than fear of something specific because it keeps us from experiencing our specific fears. Thus we never really feel clear about what we're afraid of, so we never have the opportunity to break free. When we begin to meditate, many chatty thoughts flow through our minds at the start. These arise and drift away, provided we don't latch on to them. The next layer to surface in our minds is often a layer of doubts and fears. Meditation doesn't create these feelings, they've been cowering inside us all along. All meditation does is let them rise to the surface and bubble off. Like slag from molten ore, these impurities must rise to the surface and be drained off before we can be purified. Let your thoughts and fears rise up, take a look at them and bid them bon voyage. Once we realize that our fears are not our selves, they become less frightening. Fear is just another number on the program of your life. Wouldn't you rather hear ''Blue Moon''?

Meditation provides a safe context in which to experience our thoughts and fears at a natural pace. Since no artificial stimulants are used, your own system regulates the speed at which insights arise; you never get more than you can handle. Whatever has been keeping you from enjoying the pleasure of your own company rises up and, if you don't cling to it, drifts away, never to return. That alone is worth thirty minutes a day. One of the greatest meditation masters in the world, Swami Muktananda, says this about freeing the mind in meditation:

"Let your mind spin as much as it wants to; do not try to subdue it. Simply witness the different thoughts as they arise and subside. No matter what thoughts and images arise in the mind, be aware that there is no concrete material from which they are being manifested. They are simply a phantasmagoria of consciousness, and, no matter how many worlds of desires, wishes, and positive and negative thoughts your mind creates, you should realize that they are all a play of consciousness. When thoughts or images arise in your meditation, maintain the awareness of equality—the understanding that all objects are nothing but different forms of the Self.''*

Now, after such a great build-up, surely all you want to do is head for your nearest meditation hall and sign up. Good news—you don't even have to leave your house. You have all the necessary materials already. They are your body, your mind, your true self and your willingness to learn. Although various meditation schools may disagree on some details about the meditative process, all agree that the two most important factors in meditation are posture and breath.

Posture

There are many techniques for sitting in meditation; each person finds the one most suitable to her body and temperament. Some techniques emphasize controlling the breath, some require that attention be focused on one part of the body, some claim that it's okay to move during meditation, and others insist that we should sit as still as rocks. No one technique is better or worse than another. Each individual finds the approach which is most appropriate for herself. Despite certain differences, there is one factor that every meditation school says is essential: a straight spine.

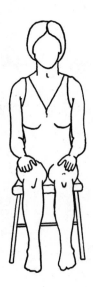

When the spine is straight we are more alert; the body is supported so that we can sit with stability and comfort for longer than five minutes. In addition to protecting the spinal cord, the spine is also the central channel of our inner energy. When it is straight and relaxed, our energy can flow freely through the body. If we perpetually slouch, the energy might still wend its way upstairs but it will be a lot harder. Why not make it easy? If your back is curved right now, sit up straight. Do you feel the difference? When the back is straight, the mind is steady.

*Meditate, by Swami Muktandanda, p. 36.

There are several meditation postures you can use which will facilitate your sitting still and straight. They are the lotus posture, the half-lotus, the "easy" posture, and the "corpse" posture. For most people, the lotus posture is the most challenging and the corpse posture is easiest. According to Patanjali, one of the most famous commentators on yoga postures, we should choose a posture which is "easy and comfortable." Although the lotus and half-lotus postures might be uncomfortable at the start, they do become extremely relaxing and comfortable after we get used to them.

Full lotus

If you want to sit in lotus posture, here's what you do. Bend the right leg at the knee. Hold the right foot with your hands and tuck it up into the root of the left thigh. Ideally, the right foot should be near the navel, but if you can't get it that high, just bring it over as far as you can. It will get easier with practice. Then pick up the left foot and place it over the right thigh in the same way. The soles of the feet should be turned up. This is the ideal meditation posture, since it locks the base of the spine, keeping it erect, and it stabilizes the body.

The half-lotus posture is similar to the lotus posture, except that you put only one leg on the opposite thigh. If you sit regularly in the lotus or the half-lotus postures, do not put the same leg up first all the time. Put the right leg up one day, and the left leg up the next. In this way your legs will develop evenly.

Half lotus

The "easy" pose is also known as "sitting cross-legged." Although this does not provide the physical stability that the lotus postures do, it is easier on the knees. If you plan to sit for extended periods of time, however, the lotus postures actually put less strain on the knees and hips. They just take longer to get used to.

If the lotus posture, the half-lotus posture, and the easy posture are all too much for you to bear, then you can resort to the "corpse" posture. If you want to feel instantly adept at yoga, start with this posture. It consists of lying flat on your back. It got its name because it was the only posture that even corpses could master. It is suitable for meditation because it guarantees that your spine will be straight. The only disadvantage of this posture is that it so closely resembles the posture we use before we fall asleep.

Cross-legged

If you use a cross-legged posture, you might find that using a small pillow to raise your hips slightly will make you more comfortable. A Japanese *zafu* is ideal for this purpose. Otherwise, any small firm pillow will do.

A few other factors will make it easier for you to meditate. It helps if you meditate in a clean, quiet place which is always set aside for meditation. You can set aside one corner of a room in which to keep your meditation cushions and clothing. If you can, it's good to wear the same clothes and use the same cushions for meditation every day. It's also helpful if you make it a habit to meditate at the same time every day, so it becomes a part of your daily routine. If you want to burn a candle or incense during meditation, that's great, too. The most important point, though, is to meditate. If you don't have special cushions or a special corner, then don't use them. If you don't have thirty minutes one day, then sit for twenty, or even ten. Daily practice is the secret to making progress in practicing meditation.

Hand Posture During Meditation

There are hundreds of different ways to hold your hands during meditation. Each of them has a subtle effect on the energy flow of your body and mind. Among all these hand postures, or *mudras*, two are fundamental. They are the *Jnana Mudra* and the *Zazen Mudra*. The *jnana* mudra is usually associated with Hindu meditation and the *zazen* mudra is usually associated with Buddhist meditation. Both of them are simple and effective.

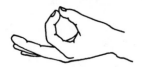

Jnana mudra

In *jnana* mudra the index finger of each hand touches the thumb in the traditional "okay" gesture. The rest of the fingers are straight but not rigid. The hands rest on the knees or thighs with the index finger touching the thumb. This is an excellent mudra for expansion and relaxation.

Zazen mudra

The *zazen* mudra is formed by placing the left palm on your open right hand. Raise both thumbs so that they touch each other lightly, forming an arch. The thumbs should touch each other firmly but without heavy pressure. Hold the hands in this position near the navel, so that the top of the thumbs rests near the navel and the palms are a few inches below the navel. Hold this mudra firmly. It grounds and focuses the mind.

Either of these mudras can carry you into meditation; choose the one that feels right to you. Whichever one you choose, use it for a while before you change to any other. That is, give it a chance to work before you send it back to the dealer.

Breath

Your breath is both the most calming tranquilizer and the most powerful stimulant in the world. Think where you'd be without it. We breathe without thinking about it, yet we can control our breath if we want to. The ability to voluntarily control our breath is the single greatest consciousness-altering technique around, and all of us have it.

When we're upset, the breath automatically becomes fast and shallow; when we're calm it becomes slow and deep. Observe your breath now. Is it deep and full, rising from the abdomen right up to the collarbone? Is it so-so, not taking any chances on busting your buttons? Or is it a collection of half-hearted little sniffs? Notice your breath. It reflects your emotional state. As in every other area of life, once you notice your unconscious breathing patterns, you can begin to change them. Take a deep breath and let all of it out. As long as there's no smog alert, you're going to feel great.

Deep, steady breath arises naturally through meditation; it is associated with a quiet mind. By knowing the connection between breath and mind, we can use the breath to still the mind. Buddhist Vipāssana meditation is based exclusively on watching the breath. After settling into your posture, you listen to the sound of the incoming and outgoing breath. Watch the breath with your inner eye as you inhale and exhale. If you become distracted, notice that you did so and then return to watching your breath. Although quite simple, the results of this meditation practice are often profound.

Another excellent way to focus the mind during meditation is by repeating a *mantra*. A *mantra* is a word which creates specific effects throughout your system. There are two kinds of *mantras*—conscious and inert. A conscious mantra is one given by a fully realized *guru* or spiritual master, and which is actively imbued with the energy of his spiritual practice. An inert *mantra* is one which is given by an incompletely trained teacher or which a person makes up for himself. True *mantras* are primordial sounds which have been passed from teacher to disciple in an unbroken line for thousands of years. By repeating a *mantra*, internally or aloud, you bring yourself closer and closer to the realization of your true self. You can repeat it during meditation and in the course of your daily life.

Either of these meditation techniques will help you stabilize your mind, and will eventually make you more intuitive. You might want to try them both and then choose the one that feels right to you, but once you've chosen a meditation technique, stick with it for a while before you change. An Indian saint named Ramakrishna once said that browsing from one spiritual practice to another is like looking for oil by digging a thousand shallow holes in a promising area. Dig until you strike oil in one and *then* see if you need to sink another well.

Although you can meditate on your own, there are significant advantages to meditating under the guidance of a teacher. There are many traditional stories about spiritual masters and their relationships with their disciples—the master-disciple relationship is probably the most intimate and profound relationship available to human beings. A true spiritual master is also called a *guru*. The word *guru* has gotten a lot of bad press recently, mostly due to the antics of would-be *gurus* who couldn't live up to their titles. A true *guru* is benign, and actually quite benevolent. The word *guru* is made of the syllables *gu* and *ru*. "*Gu*" means dispeller of darkness" and "*ru*" means darkness to light. The *guru* is the one who leads his disciples from darkness into light. True *gurus* don't demand money, death or slavering obedience from their disciples. All they ask is that their students renounce the suffering caused by their erroneous ideas about themselves and the world. And suffering is something most of us can do without.

When a student is initiated by a *guru*, his spiritual development accelerates and meditation becomes spontaneous. One of the few people now willing to give initiation, called *shaktipat*, is the Indian teacher Swami Muktananda. He teaches that "the guru is not different from the conscious Self," and that

God is immanent and can be experienced fully all the time. He gives *shaktipat* during weekend meditation intensives; his disciples also run intensives throughout the world.*

Whether you choose Buddhist or Hindu meditation, whether you go through on your own or receive the grace of a *guru*, whether you do it sitting cross-legged or on your back, meditate. The psychic skills you desire will come at their own pace, and the other benefits of meditation are inconceivable. Meditate.

Awareness in Daily Life

The Pause Button, the Troubles Game and, more than anything else, meditation, have one purpose: to make us aware of our true selves. As we look at our barriers to joy, they disappear, leaving the original pleasure of our true self shining brightly. The true self is not a prize that we get only when we meditate or say the right prayers or act like nice people. It's always there; only we aren't always looking at it. When we turn toward the joy, it is always there, no matter what we are doing.

Many tools are available to help us expand our awareness, but the most useful of them is daily life. There's certainly enough of it to work with. At every moment we can choose between the serenity and pleasure of expanded awareness or we can contract more deeply into fear. Observing ourselves is the fastest, cleanest path to expanded awareness because we can do it all the time. It is also the beginning of meditation.

Meditation does not end when we stand up after sitting still for half an hour; it only changes form. Every moment is an opportunity to deepen our meditation, every traffic ticket an interview with the *guru*. The Zen master, Hakuin, expressed the importance of practicing meditation in the midst of daily life in one of his most famous letters:

> "Yung-chia has said: 'The power of the wisdom attained by practicing meditation in the world of desire is like the lotus that rises from fire; it can never be destroyed.' Yung-chia does not mean that one should sink

---

*For more information, contact the SYDA Foundation, P.O. Box 600, South Fallsburg, N.Y. 12779.

into the world of the five desires. What he is saying is that even though one is in the midst of the five desires and the objects of the senses, one must be possessed of a mind receptive to purity, as the lotus is unstained by the mud from which it grows.

"Because the lotus that blooms in the water withers when it comes near to fire, fire is the dread enemy of the lotus. Yet the lotus that blooms from the midst of flames becomes all the more beautiful and fragrant the nearer the fire rages. . . .

"If you dauntlessly persevere in the midst of the ordinary objects of the senses, and devote yourself to pure undistracted meditation, . . . you will experience a great joy, as if you suddenly had made clear the basis of your own mind and had trampled and crushed the root of birth and death. . . . You will be like the lotus blooming from amidst the flames, whose color and fragrance become more intense the nearer the fire approaches. Why should this be so? It is because the very fire is the lotus and the very lotus is the fire."*

Daily life is meditation in disguise.

We began this book by looking at the hands, the hands that reflect our particular version of the drama of life. Moving from awareness of the hands themselves to awareness of the energy within them, we began to see the added dimensions in our hands and the hands of others. Awareness of the hands moves us to awareness of the body. Awareness of the body melts into awareness of mind, and awareness of mind becomes awareness of heart. And that's a lot of awareness.

All of this awareness is awareness with an object, that is, it's awareness *of* something or other. There is a state beyond awareness *of*, which is just plain awareness, also called pure or universal consciousness. This consciousness is the resting place of the true self, in which there is no subject and no object. From the silent marriage of subject and object springs the multiplicity of creation. Separation appears as Divine Energy spins new forms of itself to

* *The Zen Master Hakuin — Selected Writings*, P.B. Yampolsky, translator. Columbia University Press. p. 37.

play with (or against) one another. Each of us filters the cosmic light, creating from it our own lights and shadows.

Returning to this original source of consciousness, we see that the speechless Absolute is everywhere, the basis of all that is. All hands are the hands of God—none is alone. Hands clasp, hands fight, hands grip, and hands play, but the movement is nothing but one aspect of Universal Energy dancing with another. There are no other hands. If you see your friend's hands as strange, her hands will puzzle you. When you see them as aspects of your own true self, you are home. You can reflect them clearly because you know that they are not fundamentally different from your own. There are no strangers, and there are no other hands. No matter whom you're hand in hand with, you are hand in hand with your Self. That Self is sparkling consciousness and love.